FOCUS

IT'S THE PROMISE NOT THE PROCESS THAT MATTERS

DeeDee FREEMAN

FREEMAN PUBLISHING
MARYLAND

Copyright © 2016 Freeman Publishing

All rights reserved. No part of this publication may be reproduced, distributed, or transmitted in any form or by any means, including photocopying, recording, or other electronic or mechanical methods, without the prior written permission of the publisher, except in the case of brief quotations embodied in critical reviews and certain other noncommercial uses permitted by copyright law. For permission requests, write to the publisher, addressed "Attention: Permissions Coordinator," at the address below.

Freeman Publishing
2261 Oxon Run Drive
Temple Hills, MD 20748
freemanpublishing@sofcc.org

Printed in the United States of America

Scripture quotations identified NLT are from the Holy Bible, New Living Translation © 1996, 2004, 2007, 2013 by Tyndale House Foundation. Used by permission of Tyndale House Publishers Inc., Carol Stream, Illinois 60188. All rights reserved.

Scripture quotations identified NKJV are from the New King James Version®. Copyright © 1982 by Thomas Nelson. Used by permission. All rights reserved.

Scripture quotations identified AMP are from the Holy Bible, New Living Translation © 1996, 2004, 2007, 2013 by Tyndale House Foundation. Used by permission of Tyndale House Publishers Inc., Carol Stream, Illinois 60188. All rights reserved.

Scripture quotations identified MSG are from The Message. Copyright © 1993, 1994, 1995, 1996, 2000, 2001, 2002. Used by permission of NavPress Publishing Group.

Author photography by Clark Bailey Photography
Book cover design by Chantee The Designer LLC

Library of Congress Cataloging-in-Publication data
ISBN 978-1-944406-01-1

*I dedicate this book to Mike, my husband.
I can recall like it was yesterday when you thanked me for standing and believing God for you and I looked you in your eyes and said, "I only did what you taught me." Thank you for teaching me faith. I love you more than words can express. In the words of the song God gave me, "I wouldn't want to do life without you!"*

CONTENTS

ACKNOWLEDGEMENTS
INTRODUCTION

PART I: THE PROCESS
ONE: CORNERED 17
TWO: ORDERED STEPS 31
THREE: RECRUITING THE TROOPS 43
FOUR: OPERATION FAITH 57
FIVE: BELIEVERS BELIEVE 69
SIX: THE WAITING ROOM 83
SEVEN: FAITH CREDENTIALS 97

PART II: THE PROMISE
EIGHT: TRANSITION 111
NINE: THE PROMISE PERSPECTIVE 125
TEN: A PROCESS PREPARES,
A PROMISE SUSTAINS 137
ELEVEN: WELCOME HOME 155
TWELVE: FAITHFUL 167
THIRTEEN: REJOICE, RELAX & REGROUP 177

ABOUT THE AUTHOR

ACKNOWLEDGEMENTS

These acknowledgements are in no particular order

My first thanks must go to the one that gave me the ability to stand and have a testimony and that is My Father God, Himself! Then a big shout out to all of the people around the world that stood in faith with Mike and I through this process which includes our Spirit of Faith family. I pray that every dream you have comes to pass!

I am indebted to our Pastor, Apostle Fred and Betty Price for teaching us not only through precept but through demonstration in their own faith episodes on how to live by faith.

Mike, you are an awesome demonstration of strength and endurance. Thank you for not leaving me. I am one blessed woman to have such amazing children. Brittney, the way you stood with me and handled the stuff I did not want to is priceless. Brelyn thank you for giving up your comfortable bed and running through the hotel halls with me creating great memories when it seemed like a bad time. Joshua your text of love and hugs of comfort I will cherish for life. To the best in-loves Kevin, Tim, and Kesha thank you for being a great support system to all of us.

To the ones that were in the right place at the right time being led by the Spirit Himself: Keisha Williams, thank you for being led of Holy Spirit on August 22, 2014. I will never forget you. Your quick actions for your pastor saved his life. Antoinette Owens for staying at work later than usual. Dr. Sophia Smith for orchestrating the whole move to get Mike to the right place. Sophia and Richard, I do not know how you all made time for me every night but you did. Thank you just does not seem like enough.

To my family the Freemans and the Wootens, much love and appreciation for the visits. Dr. NiKia Wooten, because you suggested that we get Mike to a place that did ECMO my husband is here today. I am so proud of you. Darnice, you are everyone's dream sister. Thank you for always being here for me. I am so grateful for Dewayne and Lisa Freeman, thank you for just being you and loving me through this with your support. I love you guys deeply. Dwight and Tyrone are two of the best brother-in loves ever. Thank you for making sure I had junk to eat and I got back to the hotel safe regardless of the time.

To my friends in whom I am well pleased with. I wish everyone had friends like all of you. Cheryl Price and Angela Evans thank you for texting and calling me every single day to just talk about whatever. You guys were definitely my marathon runners. Pastor Joe and Renee Mills thank you for being there many days and late nights. Pastor Herbert and

Carol Rowe for jumping on the plane and coming to check on me.

Lastly, to the most gifted and talented people that God could connect me with: To Tressa Smallwood, of Power Play Books, thank you for making it happen! Natasha Brown for helping me to pen my words. You are phenomenal! Nikita Montgomery and Erica Berry for editing over and over and over again. Ms. Chanteé Jackson thank you for staying up late nights with me writing, making changes, designing my cover and laying out the book and all of the things I cannot remember. To all of those that I may have not put on this page but you are forever embedded in my heart.

DeeDee

INTRODUCTION
A NOTE ABOUT FAITH

When you plan out your life, you may not expect for everything to be perfect, but I am quite sure you do not plan to have to face tragedy head on. Unfortunately, tragedy was exactly what hit my family and I in the worst way. I am not certain what hell is like, and thank God I will never have to find out. But I would imagine it is a lot like watching the love of your life lie in an induced coma for almost three and a half weeks, as you hear over and over from doctors, "I am sorry, there is nothing more we can do." I would imagine hell is like watching your dreams and everything you worked to build with someone, being ripped away from you. If what I suppose is true, then it is safe to say that I have been through my own personal hell.

Have you ever gone through a process that shook you to the core and tested every ounce of strength that you had? I have, so take it from me-that is something that you would want to be prepared for. Despite this process being unwanted and unexpected, it taught me something about myself—that I am stronger than I have ever known. I learned that despite what I am facing, I am in control of the outcome. I did not just face my tragedy hoping that things would turn out in my favor; I kicked tragedy's butt! I stood like David against Goliath, defending what God told me I could have with every ounce of my strength. While I learned through my storm that I am built to last, it was not because of some superhuman ability, it was because of my faith. I like to look at it this way-all challenges are made up of three things: the problem, the process and the promise. In this threesome, one of the elements never changes. The problem may be different, and the process will likely mirror the problem, but the promise-no matter what the circumstance-never changes.

Let us look at the story of the children of Israel. They were facing a seemingly insurmountable obstacle. They had the Red Sea in front of them, and Egypt's army ready to attack behind them. I think we can call this a big problem; one that seemed impossible to survive. But God had already promised that if they trusted Him, He would not only protect them from being killed by the Egyptian army, but would perform a miracle that only He could do. The process was undoubtedly scary for some. They had to get thousands of men, women and children across the Red Sea; and believe that God would hold the water back long enough for them to make that journey safely. Is this not much like the issues you and I face? Not only do we have to believe that God will bring us out of our problem, but we have to trust Him during the process. For many of us, this is where our faith is most tested. I don't know what your problem may be. I do know that God has already released healing, prosperity, wholeness, and everything else you will ever need into the earth. What we have to do is get involved in this faith process so that we can receive the promises of God. We have to get in position to receive God's blessings, and we do so by exercising our faith.

My process required me to tap into every faith principle that I had ever learned; and because God is no respecter of persons, these faith principles are available to you as well. Although your process may differ from mine, the promise of victory is available to all who would dare to believe. I want you to know that you no longer have to suffer through painful processes, but through faith you can position yourself to walk into the promise.

After reading this book you will learn how my story ends; and you may already know how the great stories of faith in the Bible end, but what about your story? How will your story end? Will you stand in the face of tragedy or will your tragedy take you out? Will you confront adversity with courage and dignity, or will you crumble under pressure? This book is about the faith principles that saw me through the worst time in my life, and how my perspective made the difference in me being a victor rather than a victim. Often times we allow life to happen *to* us. We are passive with our dreams, our visions, and everything else that belongs to us. However, when you are in a storm, you cannot afford to be passive. You have got to put your eyes on something other than your circumstance. To go from tragedy to triumph, you have to fight fear with faith. This book will show you how to focus on the promise of victory, rather than the painful process you must endure to get there. I am a witness that when it seems like all hell is breaking loose in your life, you are in the perfect position for God to perform the miraculous on your behalf. I get to spend the rest of my life with my miracle, and everyday I am reminded of God's faithfulness. Let me tell you my story…

PART I
THE PROCESS

ONE
CORNERED

The worst conversation of my life took place on August 22, 2014. I was away on a short trip to Las Vegas with my daughter Brelyn, helping her select merchandise for her boutique. My husband, Mike, had not been feeling well that day, so I made sure I called to check on him every couple of hours. Like clockwork I reached for my phone to check in with him, but this particular call was a bit different than the previous calls. "Hey DeeDee," he murmured. It was almost as though he were whispering. I did not expect to hear such a faint voice from such a strong and robust guy. Having been married to this man for twenty-nine years, I knew immediately by his response and tone of voice that something was not quite right. He sounded so weak. I held the phone closer to my ear, struggling to hear him, and asked if he wanted me to send one of the kids to take him to the emergency room. Without hesitation, he responded, "Okay, when are they coming?" His response was an indication that this was indeed serious, and something was very wrong. Mike does not like going to the doctors' office, let alone hospitals. He would go, but it was a struggle at times getting him there. It must be a man thing, because I hear it so often about men and doctors. Let me briefly interrupt the script to encourage all men to get your annual check-ups and to respond promptly when you sense something is wrong. There are many that could be alive today if they would have gone to the doctor to address their ailments. It is disturbing for a wife to have to endure the pain of watching her husband battle an avoidable illness, all because he refused to listen to her requests to seek medical attention. Going to the doctor is not a sign that you do not have faith. In order for you to believe God you must know what you are believing Him for. I like to use this general rule- you do not ask doctors for what only God can give, and you do not ask God to do what He created doctors to do. You cannot go to your doctor and ask him to heal you because God is the Healer. But you can go to the doctor and comply with the treatment plan, so that you are in a position to receive your healing. Real men take care of themselves so they can take care of their families. I pray that this book will inspire you to take better care of your health.

You can only imagine how helpless I felt, being thousands of miles away. Anyone who knows us knows that typically if you see Mike, you see me. We truly are "joined at the hip." That being said, me being thousands of miles away in Vegas was a perfect opportunity for the enemy to attack.

I first called my son Joshua and asked him to go get his dad and take him to the emergency room. He thought I was overreacting and told me that I needed to "just relax." RELAX? If I were a cussing woman, I would have used every profane word I knew to let him know just how angry I was with him. I was furious… I mean FIRED UP! Here I am, a five-hour flight away, *my man* needs me, and you want me to chill? I wanted to beat his grown behind with a stick. I can feel the heat rising on the back of my neck as I am reliving that moment all over again, so let's move forward. Quickly realizing I needed another option, I called my oldest daughter Brittney to ask her to take her dad to the hospital. She was already on her way to check on him because she also knew he was not feeling well. When she arrived at my house, she called out to him from the outside of our bedroom and stood there awaiting his response. In the same faint voice, he told her he was getting dressed, so she gave him a few minutes. After going back and forth from our family room to the bedroom for about two hours, Mike still had not emerged from the bedroom dressed and ready to go. Brittney then called me and said that her father had not come out of the bedroom yet. Concerned, I told her to just go inside and check on him to see if he needed help. Brittney then opened the door to find her father in the bathroom, sitting on the side of the tub, looking like he was completely out of it. He was not moving, and his eyes were looking off into space. Brittney's first thought was that he might be having a stroke. While she did not panic, she knew that she had better get him help, and get it fast.

None of us knew it then, but that moment marked the beginning of our "*process*." That is the thing-when everything is great, you never consider that one day all hell will break loose. But what can you do then? As the old adage says, "You cannot build a house in a storm." The same can be said for your faith. Yet that is exactly what most find themselves trying to do when hard times come—build their faith. Your faith must be built up long before trouble comes. Because when the pressure comes and the heat is on, the only thing that you can rely on is what has been in you all along. Waiting until problems come to try and muster up the faith to endure them is impossible. It is imperative that your faith is established in Jesus when things are good, so that your foundation is sure when things are bad.

DESENSITIZED

While my family experienced one of the biggest challenges of our lives, I have had a lot of time to think about *processes*. At some point, we have all stood neck and neck with a situation that roared hopelessness, tempting us to cower into a corner. We are then left to decide whether or not we are going to allow the situation to take us out or stand flat-footed and refuse to lose. Reflecting on my response to my own process, I have in turn taken notice of how others around me respond to processes they face. I realize that our society has desensitized Christians to what it really means to go through difficult situations. Many people do not understand that they have to go through processes to see the manifested promises they are believing God for. This mindset is a bi-product of the way our society operates. We are often the victims of immediate gratification—we enjoy fast food, fast cars, fast success, and fast relationships. This in turn causes people to believe that God's timing is supposed to be the same way. As a believer, you cannot afford to entrust your hope to a timeline. Too many people start out very strong in their faith, but when things do not happen as fast as they had hoped, they abort the process. They try to manufacture microwave results, and interrupt God's plan. There are no microwave results just like there is no microwave faith. Both are contingent upon the time it takes for them to develop. *Focus* is going to slow things down a bit for you, just as it did me while I was in what appeared to be the fight of my life. Through these pages, I will share with you the emotions that my family lived through, the faith principles we maintained, and what it took to see the promise walking and talking today. You are going to learn how to focus on God's promise, and not the temporary process, when trouble comes.

AUGUST 22, 2014

I can only imagine what Brittney must have been thinking when she opened the bedroom door and saw her dad just sitting there on the side of the tub, feeble and unable to move. Was he having a stroke? A seizure? ... After a few unsuccessful attempts to help her father up, she called her husband Kevin from the family room to come and help her take Mike to the hospital. Mike was fussing and complaining that he did not want Kevin's help. My husband is a very private and dignified man when it comes to his health, and he did not want Kevin's help because he was convinced that he could manage on his own. Fortunately, they ignored his complaints and focused on getting him out of the house as quick as possible. With all of their strength, my daughter and son-in-law walked Mike out of the house and rushed him to the nearest urgent care facility. The whole way, his speech was irrational and they could not understand a thing he was saying. When they arrived, a member of our church, Keshia, who happened to be the x-ray tech on duty, recognized Mike in the waiting room and immediately rushed him back to check his oxygen level. It was at 22%, much lower than the standard of 93% or above. This explained his crazy speech. His brain was in desperate need of oxygen. They put Mike on 100% oxygen, and finally got his up to 70%. Once he was stabilized, Keisha, directing the Urgent Care staff, called the ambulance to take him to the local community hospital. My husband was then transported to the intensive care unit at the local community hospital where he lay in critical condition. At this point, the doctors and nurses thought Mike-my strong, robust husband-was a dead man.

I was still in Vegas, but I was scheduled to leave late that night. I could not find an earlier flight to save my life. I searched and searched, but nothing was available. It had been hours since I heard my husband's voice on the phone, and I was becoming more and more anxious to be with him. The last time I would hear from Mike that day was later on that evening. He sent me a picture of himself wearing an oxygen mask, with a text that said, "I'm okay." I texted him back and said, "I know you are." I knew Mike was ill, but I also knew that the only power I had from

Vegas was praying power, which is the best power, so I simply trusted God. After receiving his text, and fortifying my faith in God to take care of him better than I ever could, I went shopping with my daughter Brelyn and Tam, a family friend and partner of our church. This is the first lesson for you to remember about being in a faith process-*keep calm and trust God*. When we truly trust Him and have faith in His promises, our actions align with our beliefs. So many people, when faced with adversity, crawl in bed, draw the curtains, and isolate themselves from others. This is exactly the position the enemy wants you to take. His goal is to get you to focus on your problem so that you begin to rehearse and meditate on every negative scenario. The enemy knows that once it becomes real to your emotions, it will translate into your thoughts, which affect the things you say, which ultimately end up manifesting in your life. It is important not to trip out and start acting crazy when it looks like the devil has knocked us down. To me, everything *was normal* in the spiritual world (in which I operate)—even if my natural world was turned upside down. God had it covered. So until I could catch a flight home, I shopped in peace, knowing that my Father's promise would prevail.

FAITH OVER STATISTICS

I was finally able to book a flight around 8 p.m. We flew into BWI Airport, and I arrived at the hospital between 3 and 4 a.m. Mike was not breathing well at all. I could look at him and tell that he was not able to take in the oxygen he needed. They had the machine pumping out oxygen at 100%, but it just was not working. That morning, the doctors came in and insisted he be intubated, but he refused. He was fighting the machines, and was now "oxygen hungry," a condition referred to as dyspnea-a disorder associated with impaired breathing. After much prodding, Mike finally agreed to intubation and was immediately rushed into surgery. The x-rays showed that both of his lungs were whited out—meaning he had no air space at all. My niece Dr. Nikia Wooten, an emergency room physician at another hospital, came and examined the x-rays and met with the doctors. At this point, the attendant on duty had a very serious, and what he thought was a "professional" conversation with her. "You need to prepare your family for the worst. You are a medical professional, and you cannot give them false hope. We both know where this goes from here," he said. She gasped, taken aback by his comment. There was conflict between her knowledge as a medical professional, her emotional investment because the patient was also her family member, and what the Bible says about what to do in times of trouble. She was in an extremely tough position. She had to go against her better judgment as a medical professional, and instead be led by her spiritual convictions. And this, for a medical doctor, is more than a test of their faith-it's an ethical dilemma. She had a huge fight on her hands. She had the menacing voice of negative statistics to combat. She knew she had never seen anyone recover from the state that Mike was in. As a medical professional, she knew she had to be realistic, but as a *believer who walks in faith*, she could not tell us—her family—that the physicians said Mike was going to die. So the only thing left to do was stand on her faith. Nikia has been a member of our church since she was a teenager. What she knows about faith is largely attributed to what she heard us teach. It is amazing how things come full circle. If we had not been teachers of faith, she would not have been able to stand, which would have made her extremely vulnerable to her colleague's recommendation. I'm so glad that we were obedient to God and faithful to His Word even in building the faith of those who depend on us for spiritual guidance.

When Nikia came back to speak with us, she told Brittney and I that the situation did not look good, and it was very serious. It was going to be an uphill battle. Yet, instead of giving up hope, my niece made a medical decision and insisted that we get Mike out of that hospital quickly. "We need a hospital with an ECMO[1] machine" she shared. The medical attendant wanted Mike to stay there for 24 hours because they had just intubated him, but Nikia insisted that we did not have 24 hours. If we did not act fast, his condition would decline. While her recommendation could have been perceived as undermining to the attending doctor's knowledge and skill, my niece had to be willing to stand on what she knew. This was a dangerous position to be in because the doctor could have been so bent on defending his pride that he was unwilling to go along with her suggestion and kept Mike at his facility. The hospital's resources were clearly tapped out, and we needed to have him transferred to a facility that could save his life immediately. However, when my niece shared with us that it was time to go to a hospital that was better equipped to help Mike, I had the total peace of God; which is why I was confident in moving him, despite the attending doctor's recommandation. Listen, my faith was not in that machine, but in God.

The devil thought he had us cornered. He was probably dancing and partying in hell because he *just knew* one of God's generals was down. Our backs were truly up against the wall, in the natural, but that

---

1   Extracorporeal membrane oxygenation (ECMO) is an extracorporeal technique of providing both cardiac and respiratory support to persons whose heart and lungs are unable to provide an adequate amount of gas exchange to sustain life.

corner would not remain our post. I still had some fight in me, and God knows I would need it for what was coming next.

FAITH PRINCIPLE ONE

Keep calm and trust God.

When you trust Him, and have faith in His promises, you will not panic when it looks like the devil has you cornered.

I want you to think about your life, as it is right now. What situation could be an indication that you are in "A Faith Process"? Have you found yourself in a corner? What actions could you take to trust God and stay calm, despite what things look like in the natural?

WORD WEAPON

Fear not [there is nothing to fear], for I am with you; do not look around you in terror and be dismayed, for I am your God. I will strengthen and harden you to difficulties, yes, I will help you; yes, I will hold you up and retain you with My [victorious] right hand of rightness and justice.

Isaiah 41:10 AMP

TWO
ORDERED STEPS

I felt like I was in one of Stephen King's thrillers— and yet I remained calm. The mood at the local hospital was extremely tense. They could not get Mike's oxygen level stable, they were failing to get air to his brain, and they became perplexed trying to figure out how to stabilize him. There were so many things that they "could not do" there. The doctors were not saying what we needed to hear, and I could tell they lacked faith in themselves that they could do what needed to be done to keep him alive. People kept warning us about the worst, as we were trusting God for the best. Things just were not going well, but we decided to trust the Word of God, "What is impossible with men is possible with God." Luke 18:27. Once my niece, Dr. Nikia, ensured us that we needed to have Mike transferred to another hospital with an ECMO machine, the countdown was on. My faith was on, and my resolve to see my husband out of this hospital bed and back to his normal self was on. I had no clue what "ECMO" was, but because Nikia recommended that this was what Mike needed, I went along with the decision to transfer him confident in my inner man that it was indeed time to go.

GOD MET THIS DAY BEFORE YOU DID…

When I tell you the hand of God orchestrated everything, you had better believe it. What happened next was crazy. My niece called another physician, Dr. Sophia Smith, MD, and informed her of Mike's situation. Dr. Sophia is a partner of our church, and she immediately got the ball rolling. Dr. Sophia called her sister Toni, who was a nurse at Washington Hospital Center. Toni then connected us to Dr. Molina, the only doctor at the hospital who could make a decision to place patients on the ECMO machine. He just so happened to be in surgery at that time. I am trying to paint a picture here, because oftentimes we think we have to work things out, when God has already worked it out. All you have to do is trust that God has already met this day before it came in contact with you. He has already orchestrated the affairs to work out in your favor. My niece, Nikia did not know that Dr. Sophia and

Toni knew Dr. Molina. Furthermore, Toni, Dr. Sophia's sister, was not even supposed to be at work when that call came. She only stayed late to handle some things that she typically would have waited to do the next day. In addition, Dr. Molina just happened to be doing the same procedure on another patient at the exact time we were inquiring about his ability to help Mike. Some would say that all these things were just "coincidences", but I challenge you as a believer to understand that nothing "just happens." Everyone's steps were just as the Lord ordered them. From Brittney getting to her dad just in time, to Keisha being on duty in the urgent care at the front desk when Mike came in, to Dr. Nikia realizing that Mike needed to be moved to a hospital with ECMO, to Dr. Sophia calling her sister, and then the only physician with the authority to authorize ECMO being on duty… God worked it all out. Toni and Dr. Sophia spoke with a transport specialist who assured them that Mike could be transported in a matter of hours. Despite the local hospital's objections, and their warnings of the high risk of potential death if they moved Mike, we were sure this was the way to go. Within four hours, Washington Hospital Center sent a medevac, and Mike was on his way.

STAY STEADY

That night, Brelyn was having a Girls Night Out at her store,

Breezy's Boutique. I was scheduled to minister to an eager group of ladies at this event. Some of our loved ones suggested that I cancel my appearance, but I refused to let the enemy ruin any more of God's plans. I left two of our best friends, the Mills, at the hospital to see my husband off to the other facility. Meanwhile, I did the only thing I knew to do- trust God and keep going. I was not scared and I did not doubt for one second that Mike would survive. While we were laughing and having an amazing time pouring into the young women that night, the medevac pilot told our friends "He probably will not make it." I was furious when I learned of this. Why would they say that about a patient? After I heard this, I knew that God had me right where He wanted me that night, because there is no telling what I would have done to that pilot had he said that in front of me. As soon as the event was over, I had my friend Tam take me to the new hospital where Mike had been sent. She had no idea what was transpiring. Closing the car door, I turned to her and said, "Tam, Pastor Mike has been medevacked to the hospital." Tam was shocked at my calm demeanor and that I even spoke at the Girls Night Out like nothing was going on. Throughout this whole process, I was determined to remain the same. If nothing else resonates with you, I want you to highlight and absorb the following lesson into your spirit: The greatest indication that you are not in faith is that you are no longer able to operate in a clear and level-headed manner. You will start adapting to what you are going through, instead of allowing what you are going through to adapt to you.

When I arrived at the hospital, Mike was in a pronator bed—which looked like a giant sandwich that covered him from top to bottom. I could only see his shoulders. The bed flipped him upside down in an attempt to get his lungs off of his back. He tolerated the machine fairly well for about four hours. But after that, his numbers dropped to extremely critical rates, and his blood pressure started to rise higher and higher. The hospital tested Mike for everything, but could not find a thing that would have caused his body react this way. They tested to see if it was viral or bacterial. They had to give it a name, so it was labeled as *Acute Respiratory Distress Syndrome*, an umbrella category for any attack of the lungs. When the pronator bed failed to work, the doctor returned defeated stating, "Things do not look good. His lungs are clouded." He explained how terrible Mike's x-rays were. When you see your lungs on an x-ray machine, you should see black, which means that air is coming through. Mike's lungs were all white. He was getting progressively worse, and no one who was there in the natural seemed to have anything positive to say about his situation.

The doctor continued with, "If ECMO does not work, nothing

will." They took him out of the Pronator Bed, and decided that he needed to be on the ECMO machine-*and fast!* I never panicked or worried when the pronator bed did not work. This ECMO machine was the solution. That was the vehicle to the promise that we were believing God for-healing, despite what things looked like in the natural. Remember when we were at the local hospital? Despite the bleakness of the situation, and the attendant predicting Mike's death, my niece refused to deliver that news to us—instead, she allowed the Holy Spirit to breath into her another option—ECMO. So although the doctors at Washington Hospital Center began to panic over their first failed treatment strategy—GOD had already told us to go to that hospital for ECMO. I really hope you are following this in a spiritual sense. There was no time to panic, God had just used that doctor to echo what we already knew—ECMO was a key factor of the promise.

  Brittney, her husband, and I were together in the waiting room. We waited about three hours for the doctor to meet us because he was in surgery with another patient, who sadly died while on the ECMO machine. You would think that news would have crushed our optimism but as far as we were concerned, that situation, while unfortunate, had nothing to do with us. We had laser focus and could not be moved. Like a team strategizing the next play, we revisited the planning process and discussed the course of action before the doctor came in the room. When the doctor finished describing the severity of Mike's situation, he said, "ECMO is a last-ditch effort." Brittney, without hesitation, told him that we wanted to proceed with ECMO, and I was fully confident in her ability to make the right decision. We signed the papers for the ECMO procedure, and within a couple of hours, he was in surgery. Before the procedure began, we prayed with all the physicians that the wisdom of God would be released in their lives and that God would reveal exactly what they needed to do to treat Mike. Truthfully speaking, Brittney and I were detached from the natural scenario. The doctors were thinking we were not being realistic concerning Mike's condition, but that could not have been further from the truth. We knew what it looked like, but our minds were set on the end result. "We got this," Brittney and I assured each other, as we continued to wait.

While Mike was on the ECMO machine, his condition began to improve. At one point, we were told that he was breathing alright, but there were some dangerous levels of carbon dioxide in his lungs. This too was very serious and life threatening. If I were not a woman of faith, I might have panicked, because every time one thing started to work, it seemed like something else happened that threatened to take us out of the game. Although I was furious with the devil, we continued to believe God for the end result, and remained calm. The next day, the physician told us that they were trying a new drug—and this was a one shot deal to get his carbon dioxide to appropriate levels. Well that one shot worked, and from that point on, Mike's body did not have any problems with carbon dioxide.

    After three weeks in, I remember learning that one ICU physician would be on duty for seven days straight. He told me that he did not know what they would do, or how this treatment would end up. In the beginning, he was not confident at all that they could stabilize my husband and save his life. So I prayed with him that God would show him some unconventional ideas and means of getting the job done. I prayed and declared that the wisdom of God would begin to tell him things that he may not naturally think to do. I told all the doctors who crossed our paths that I did not want my husband to be treated based on numbers or case studies. I wanted him to be treated as an individual. Mike was a totally different case. I knew that, I just needed the doctors to agree. I needed those doctors to look at his body and know exactly what to do for him specifically.

    During every shift I would go into Mike's room. Every time a new doctor or nurse came in, I would pray with them first, prior to them checking on him, touching him, or explaining anything to me. I needed them to know that we were operating in faith. "Are you getting ready to touch him?" I asked each nurse and doctor. "Let me pray with you first." At one point the hospital chaplain came in and he wanted to pray over Mike, and I told him, "No that's okay." I rejected because I did not know what he would pray. You have to be bold enough to stand up to protect what belongs to you. I was not going to allow this man to pray just because he was the chaplain of the hospital, just to be nice. This was serious business-spiritual warfare. I was not spooky about it at all, but I had to be sure that these doctors and medical professionals were a part of our army.

At the end of the third week, on a Friday, the ICU doctor, whom we had prayed with, told me that he decided to do something "unconventional"-the exact word I used when praying with him. They started a procedure where they began to take a tube to wash out his lungs with saline. That procedure began to break up all of the junk and mucus that was in his lungs, which would eventually improve his breathing and make it possible for him to breath on his own again. That moment was a major turning point for us. Finally, the doctors were confident that things were going in the right direction, because they began to see more air space in Mike's lungs. "On Monday, I did not know how things would go; but today, I am sure things are moving in the right direction," the physician said. All I could do was praise God! Our last-ditch efforts and unconventional, intense prayers were lining up with our faith confession!

FAITH PRINCIPLE TWO

Remain steady.

You will know when you are not operating in faith, because you start to change things up when things begin to look bad. Instead of switching your routine, stand in faith and allow God to guide your steps remembering that He has met this day before you and has set the course for your victory.

What are some of the promises that God has ministered to you through His Word regarding what you are facing? You will need to meditate on these scriptures to remain steady and unmoved as you face this challenge.

WORD WEAPON

So my dear brothers and sisters, stand strong. Do not let anything change you. Always give yourselves fully to the work of the Lord, because you know that your work in the Lord is never wasted.

I Corinthians 15:58 NCV

THREE
RECRUITING THE TROOPS

Once I realized we were in for a long process, I was prepared for war. I told the doctors that I was in it for the long haul, and no matter if it took one big "Hail Mary" to get us in the end zone, or several small important plays, I was willing to fight for this victory.

I immediately identified the people that I could call on to pray and stand with me. This was a war, and I needed the strongest troops in my army on board. So I called on friends across this nation to conduct spiritual warfare on Mike's behalf. Make a note of this strategy of war–size up your troops! Choosing the right troop is an important factor when focusing on the promise over the process. Figure out how spiritually strong your circle is. Your good girlfriend may not be the one to call on during a battle. She may be good for shopping, and that may be it. Your buddy may be good for playing ball, but you must size him up to see if he is ready for an all out spiritual war. When you are in a fight, you have to know who can go to war with you. Furthermore, you cannot be afraid to get rid of the people in your life that do not qualify for your battle. There is a story in the Bible that comes to mind. In the book of Judges, a man named Gideon was preparing for battle. He had 32,000 soldiers and was pretty confident in his ability to go against the opposing army. But the Lord told him he had too many. So the army was reduced to 10,000 solders, sending the other 22,000 home. Then God said that Gideon still had too many soldiers. Finally, Gideon's army was reduced to a mere 300 men, and at that point, God told him that he was now ready to face his opponent. Gideon did not need a whole host of people fighting with him. He needed the God-ordained ones that qualified to stand with him in the battle, knowing that at the end of it all, only God could take credit for the victory. Just like Gideon in this story, I did not need a whole bunch of soldiers. I just needed the ones that I identified as ones who were qualified to fight with me. I needed to know that they knew what I believed and would be able to flow with me, knowing that in the end, God alone would get the glory.

    The weapons of warfare are meditating in the Word, prayer and worship! It is critical that you identify the spiritual strengths in the people that you associate with when all is well because you cannot build a house in a storm. So while things are on the up and up, Develop relationships with people you know that pray and would intercede for you. You can identify prayer warriors as soon as you tell them to pray for you. Look at their response. If they begin to ask you a bunch of questions to see exactly what is going on in your life, and why they need to pray for you, they may not be fit for your battle. You do not need to know what a person is going through in order to pray for them. The Bible says in Romans 8:26, 'Likewise the Spirit also helps in our weaknesses. For we do not know what we should pray for as we ought, but the Spirit Himself makes intercession for us with groanings which cannot be uttered.' Equally, has anyone ever asked you to pray for them, only for you to say, "Okay," and walk away forgetting all about them? Start a habit to stop what you are doing to pray for that person right there. It is easy to forget if you do not do it then. Biblical meditation, prayer and worship will be your greatest weapons during a battle. Understand that as a Christian, you are in constant spiritual warfare, and the only way to fight a spiritual war is through the spirit—and with Holy Spirit-filled troops by your side.

STRATEGIC AMBUSH

In my case, as the situation progressed, I had everyone focus, through prayer, on specific challenge areas, and we targeted those areas all at the same time. I identified my sprinters and my marathon runners. Both roles are needed just like on a track team. I did not minimize anyone's role. However, it is necessary to distinguish which individuals belong to which group, so that you will not have false expectations about who will be around for the long haul or short term. All of my troops were truly spirit fighters. I would call on the same people if I ever need them again. Some of the people I called on to pray are not people who I talk to on a regular basis. These were people that Mike and I had connected with over the years. I went outside of my circle to identify some of my prayer warriors, but I knew for a fact that their spiritual walks had produced fruit. So after I knew each person's role, I was confident that we were ready to battle our greatest enemy. We took our positions and prepared for a strategic ambush.

When Mike went into the hospital, I sent out a general text asking our family and friends to come in agreement with me for Mike's health. I let them know his lungs were attacked and he was in the hospital. I also gave them Amos 9:13 in the Message Bible to pray and meditate on, and declare and decree over Mike's life:

"Yes indeed, it won't be long now." God's Decree. "Things are going to happen so fast your head will swim, one thing fast on the heels of the other. You won't be able to keep up. Everything will be happening at once—and everywhere you look, blessings! Blessings like wine pouring off the mountains and hills. I'll make everything right again for my people Israel: "They'll rebuild their ruined cities. They'll plant vineyards and drink good wine. They'll work their gardens and eat fresh vegetables. And I'll plant them, plant them on their own land. They'll never again be uprooted from the land I've given them." God, your God, says so."

Whew! Now that is a powerful passage. Imagine the impact we made against the kingdom of darkness, with all of us spirit fighters praying that Word over this attack. Healing would happen at once, and *everywhere we looked... blessings!* That was another promise that all of the soldiers fighting alongside of me in this battle believed God for and we decreed and declared this Word for our lives and blessings over Mike's body.

No one asked me any questions. They all jumped right on it.

And the troops were released in a strategic way to ambush the enemy's plan. When I received good or bad reports, I sent them updates about what was going on, so they could target certain areas with me (including the medical professionals who were working on Mike, a specific pain he had, various things we were in need of, etc.). We also covered specific medical procedures with prayer, in advance. I believe this very strategic approach to our process helped us tremendously. We prayed circles around the areas in Mike's body that the devil tried to attack, and believed God! The Bible says in James 5:16, '... *Pray for one another, that you may be healed. The effective, fervent prayer of a righteous man avails much.*' The word fervent means intense and passionate. There is power and healing waiting to be unlocked through your prayers. So you better believe that having an army of troops who know how to pray, and whose prayers are all focused and intense, will penetrate the gates of hell.

FAMILY ROLES

This process helped me to identify strengths in my children and it brought them closer spiritually. They each had a specific and important role to play, and no matter how big or small, I embraced and appreciated them for the parts they played. Mike being down made us all pull together, and operate in the faith that he has taught us.

Brittney

Brittney is my faith baby. Growing up, this girl would believe God for the color of bubble gum balls that she wanted out of the machine. I would stand behind her hoping and praying that she would get what she wanted. Without fail, she would get the exact color bubblegum ball she believed God for. The seeds of faith were planted in her early, and today, she has a major harvest of answered prayers to solidify her identity as a faith warrior. Her faith has always been on fire, so to have her with me through this process was truly a blessing.

Brittney was my right-hand soldier during this process, and her faith was as strong as mine. I recall a day when we were at the local hospital. The primary doctor who was caring for Mike met with us at one point, and kept saying, "He is as sick as he can be." After he said that phrase one too many times, Britt stopped him, and told him not to ever say that again. She explained, "My dad is not as sick as he can be." Brittney is strong, bold and very confident in the Word. She will not allow you to say anything contrary to what she is believing God for. Just like me, Brittney was strong in her faith and it was visible through her actions. She was the one who wanted to know all the details about every prescription, machine and procedure concerning her dad. The doctors and nurses were all very impressed with how she knew all that information "to a T". She would often tell me that she had Power of Attorney over *my husband*. That girl is hilarious. I never saw Brittney buckle in her faith. She would come and hang out at the hospital with her family, and just keep me company sometimes. Thinking of the role that Brittney played reminds me of a very important point in the art of spiritual warfare—your leaders on the front line will step up automatically. It will be natural to them. Every general needs a lieutenant like her.

    Brittney did not become one of my most reliable and faith-filled soldiers, without having to endure some battles of her own. I have seen her go through her own faith fights where she had to believe God's promises, despite the processes she was in. One that stands out the most is when she was pregnant with her twins. The doctor instructed Brittney to abort one of the babies (Demi), because she was critically ill and would die, and also kill Dakota. To make a long story short, Brittney refused, and instead trusted God through the whole process. The doctor who advised her to abort was a part of the delivery team for my little grand-kisses. God orchestrated it so that he would have a front row seat to her triumphant faith fight. They were both born alive and healthy and are the two sweetest blessings in our family. Brittney's faith saved Demi and Dakota. She can pray for me anytime!

Joshua

At one point, my son thought his dad was going to die. I had no idea of this at the time, but he later said this one Sunday while ministering at church. Yet, in this process, he played the role of the encourager.

I remember receiving a group text that Joshua sent to the girls and I thanking us and telling us how much he loved us. He would come to the hospital just to hang out. He took us all out to lunch one day, and went to dinner with us at other times. Joshua came to the hospital when Mike was in ICU only to see and support me. He does not do well seeing someone he loves sick or in the hospital. After four weeks, Josh decided to go in the room, because his dad was awake. Mike was still a bit out of it due to all of the drugs they had him on, but Josh felt that he was finally ready to see him. However, when Josh went into the room, he could not handle seeing his father in such a seemingly helpless position, so he walked out. The next time he saw his dad was during a conversation over FaceTime, when Mike first started to speak again. Later, after all was well, Josh shared how he did not want to see his dad in that condition, and that he feared the worst—that it would be his last time seeing him, and he did not want to have to remember him in that way.

I knew Josh's faith was not the same as mine. He was in the fight, but he fought differently so I did not want him in the room. He never received any pressure from me. All of my children were troopers, and each trooper had a role. Josh's role was to send love messages, and believe me-I cherished every text I received from him. He was my emotional support.

Brelyn

All of my children handle challenges differently. Brelyn is smack dab in the middle of Joshua and Brittney. She will appear to be strong, but in actuality she may not be as strong as she seems. There is a certain dignity that Brelyn walks in because she understands her role as an example to others. During this process, Brelyn was with me the most because she was single at the time, and could stay with me over night. When I knew that Mike would be at a particular hospital for a length of time, I decided to get a hotel room near the hospital, so that I could be closer to him without having to endure a long commute. Brelyn would stay with me at the hotel to make sure that I was all right. It took Bre two to three weeks to get herself ready to see her dad. The first time she decided she was going to see him, she was in the waiting room with some of our other family members, and was sitting on the floor. All of a sudden, she jumped up and said, "Okay I'm ready." Brittney took her in the room and when they got in there, the nurse said, "Oh I was just about to clean him up…" Well, Brelyn used that as her excuse to scurry out of the room. She was only in there a few seconds. While her dad was in ICU, she probably saw him six or seven times within the six-week period. Throughout this entire process, she would send our immediate family text messages, a scripture and a prayer to focus on for the day. She would be so on point, that we would tease her saying we didn't realize she knew the Bible so well.

One day after Mike was in ICU for about four weeks, Brelyn came to the hospital and sat in the room, with a distant look on her face. I leaned over and asked what was going on. She looked at me, with weariness written all over her face and said, "I just want him to get up so we can go home." I wanted the same thing, but I was in for the long haul, so it did not matter to me how long it took.

"Come on let's go," I told her, and we went for a walk. We went to the chapel and we prayed and sang worship songs. When we left the hospital chapel, she was a new girl. I never saw her draw back to that place again. She still did not go in the room every time she came, but that was perfectly fine.

It is important not to allow others to push you pass your own faith level. My children were given the liberty to handle their dad's situation in their own ways, without any pressure from me. As a matter of fact, in the beginning, I only allowed my brother-in-law DeWayne and his wife Lisa to come into the ICU room. I kept everyone else out, including Mike's parents. I was not sure how others would have handled seeing Mike in that state. I had nothing against them personally; I was just on a mission and had to make some tough decisions along the way. They were not my focus. I had one thing on my mind and that was to protect and guard my interest. Do not be so loyal to people that you cannot stand up for what is necessary for you and your peace. During the process, never allow anyone to overstep your boundaries. Once you recruit the troops, and identify everyone's role, you have to ensure they are all working in accordance with the plan you have laid out to reach your promise. Certainly, with the troops in place, the devil was sweating as we walked out of the corner he thought he had us backed into. We were determined to keep moving towards the promise ordered by God Himself.

FAITH PRINCIPLE THREE

Identify the faith troop & their roles.

Figure out who can go to (spiritual) war with you. Determine whom your prayer warriors are, who is good for encouragement, and who can take your mind off the natural. Figure out each person's role during your process, and get ready for war. Mobilize the troops with strategic prayer and worship and do not forget to declare and decree God's promises (from His Word) over your process!

For that process that you are in now, take a moment to jot down who can go to war with you and how, and begin connecting with them. Then begin to read God's Word, faithfully, and highlight any promises from Him that jump off the pages and into your spirit. It's wartime!

WORD WEAPON

Fulfill my joy by being like-minded, having the same love, being of one accord, of one mind.

Philippians 2:2

FOUR
OPERATION FAITH

At this point I hope you have taken time to catch your breath and calm down, fixed your heart on the promises of God for your situation, and identified your troops. Remember, we are in this for the long haul so we have curbed fear and we are not concerned about how long our process takes. We are standing fixed on seeing the manifested promise of God, and everything around us has to align with that. Our faith has taken center stage.

Earlier, I mentioned how the local hospital workers had very little faith in their ability to treat Mike, and I also shared how various medical professionals spoke negatively about his condition. We had to change the atmosphere to get him in the presence of doctors who believed they could treat him. They did not believe at first, but we changed their minds by our faith. No, we did not blast gospel music in the waiting rooms, and we did not bully doctors and nurses into receiving Jesus. We believed and our words and actions changed the atmosphere. We would pray and what we prayed for would come to pass. They had no choice but to believe. We brought the presence of God and the Holy Spirit into our natural atmosphere. I declared "Operation Faith" in full effect.

> *"He did not waver at the promise of God through unbelief, but was strengthened in faith, giving glory to God, and being fully convinced that what He had promised He was also able to perform."*
>
> Romans 4:20-21

The response of Abraham to the PROMISE he had been given jumped into my spirit! During the fight of our lives, I recalled how Abraham operated while he was waiting for God to deliver on His promise to bless him with a child. The likelihood of Abraham and Sarah conceiving a child seemed weak, but God delivered on His Word. The life of my husband was no different to me. I declared, "God, either your Word is true or it is not. I have been doing this for a long time, and I know that if You have been faithful over the small things, You will be faithful over the big things." Both Mike and I have lived and walked by faith, and we were certain of God's promises for our lives. Mike has said, "God is not a respecter of persons, but He is a respecter of faith." I knew that I could count on God to bring us through, and so I did not entertain unbelief regardless of the facts. Just as Abraham, I was convinced. I continued to feed my spirit man with the Word of God and became strengthened in faith. As we feed our spirit, the Holy Spirit will tell us what to do, what to say, and what to pray.

CHANGE THE ATMOSPHERE

"On Monday, I didn't know how things would go, but today, I'm sure things are moving in the right direction," the physician said....

Eventually, we had all of the doctors in agreement with what we were believing, because of how firm we stood. I told them that even though I knew they had to give me the information and their perspective of Mike's health, I had written my own script for how this whole thing was going to go, and it was going to turn out in my favor. One by one, they all came in agreement with me, and never said anything to oppose my faith. I changed the atmosphere by speaking faith-filled words, and those words transformed unbelievers into believers when it was all said and done.

Part of my means to change the atmosphere and set the tone was to videotape all of the positive feedback from the nurses and physicians and send it back to my troop. If the doctors said something positive, I had them repeat it for video. Mike was unconscious and was not responding to our voices or even the procedures for some time. I wanted to shape their perceptions, and continue feeding them the positive news, despite any downturns that showed up along the way. I needed them to internalize the positive end result, so that when they actually saw Mike, despite how bad he really looked, they would believe what they could not see. I stood firm in not letting anyone come in the room who could not handle Mike's natural state. Operation Faith was in effect, not just for Mike's healing, but for our spiritual state as well. When we talk about Operation Faith, it is just like training for anything else. Everyone in training may have the same muscles, but some people's muscles are developed more than others. This is how faith works. Each of us has been given a measure of faith (Rom. 12:3), and some of us have faith that is more developed than others. As a part of my strategy, I had to build the faith of others who were fighting with me during this time.

People tell me that the mental toughness I displayed was remarkable, and it was to me as well. I did not realize how strong I was until I went through this process. People who came around me constantly asked how I was able to stand so strong during this trying time. Truthfully, I do not do well with seeing others in pain. If you were to tell me your leg hurts, my leg would begin to hurt too. That is taking empathy a little too far, I know. I remember the first time I saw the doctors and nurses clear out Mike's lungs. He was sedated, and he began to gag and cough. His entire body seemed to convulse and jump up off of the bed. I immediately excused myself from the room, because I did not want to create any negative images for my mind and spirit to meditate on. Over time, I exposed myself to his process and treatment in little doses at a time. Eventually, I became immune to seeing things like that, and it no longer bothered me.

IT'S ALL ABOUT PERSPECTIVE

If you allow the bad that is happening in the natural world to shape your perspective, you will not operate in faith. I knew this, not only for myself, but for our loved ones as well. My perspective came from the Word of God. I allowed God's Word to shape my perspective and what I believed, and a lot of people did not understand that, but it is the truth.

I had done so well at shaping the perspectives of those around us, that I had some explaining to do after a while. There were a few friends from out of town that I had been talking with the entire time. One of those special people was our spiritual covering Apostle Frederick K.C. Price, who flew in from California to visit Mike. I had been sending updates to him, his wife and his daughter. But again, everyone received updates based on the perspective that I saw. The only picture anyone had was the picture that I gave them, and you already know I was committed to sharing positive reports. I remember Apostle Price, his wife Betty, and his daughter Angie came into town, and arrived at the hospital. I met them downstairs when they got out of the car. I told them that I would take them upstairs, but first I wanted to give them an update regarding what Mike looked like. I knew they would be in for a shock if I did not explain what they were about to see because Mike looked worse than what they knew. I never lied to anyone about what was going on but I never described every detail of how he looked. Many believers get this particular process confused. The Scripture says that we call those things that be not as though they were. We do not call those things that are, as though they are not. Let me make this plain. I never said Mike is not sick. I knew he was sick. Everyone around me knew he was sick. For me to say he was not sick when he was, would have been me calling those things that be, as though they are not. I am not telling you to say you are not sick when you are. I am telling you to call yourself healed while there is sickness in your body. Because calling yourself healed, though you are sick, is calling those things which be not as though they were. Apostle Price kindly brushed me off, in his loving way, and said, "We're used to this. Let's go and see Mike." So we proceeded to go into Mike's room. They opened the door and walked in, and I heard Apostle Price moan, "Oh Michael," as if he was in shock. He was surprised that Mike looked so bad, because I had never given them any indication that his visual state was as bad as it was. When I shared updates with him, I would never say, "Oh he's not doing good," nor did I ever say, "he isn't looking so well today." Everyone who saw him once I finally loosened the reigns was surprised by the magnitude of Mike's sickness.

Mike also had a friend who would call me everyday and ask me, "How is he doing now?" And I would say, "He is doing the same way he was doing the last time I talked to you." He would call me maybe every hour for a period of time. Finally, after Mike got better, he told us, that he could not figure out how I was doing so well, when I told him exactly what Mike was going through. His sister had pneumonia, and he remembered how he felt, going through it with her. He just could not understand why I did not feel the same way he had felt.

Mike was in ICU for a total of six weeks, and while he was in the hospital, I spent most of my time in the waiting room with my friends and family and doing schoolwork. All the doctors and nurses knew exactly where I was. I would go in the room for a few minutes at a time, when he first went in, just to touch him and talk to him, so he could hear my voice. As the weeks progressed, I would stay longer. I didn't want to give my flesh any opportunity to oppose my faith. In order to stay grounded and believe in the promise, I could not just sit there and look at him in that unproductive state. While I was in the waiting room, I could picture whatever I wanted to. At one point, someone tried to tell me that I needed to be in the room with Mike more, but I found out I was in charge, whether I was in the room with Mike or in the waiting room… and I am not talking about "in charge" of the physical space. I am talking about the spiritual.

If you are implementing your own Operation Faith, realize that you have to continue to be the primary believer, the general, and champion of God's promise. This means that you have to protect your mental state and your physical space. Do not expose yourself to more than your flesh can handle, and always feed your spirit and starve your flesh. Remove yourself from faithless environments. I refused to cry because I knew if I allowed myself over in that arena I may not bounce back. I protected my own imagination by limiting my time in his hospital room. These decisions, in addition to the belief I had in God's promises, made it possible for me to believe things that I did not see. And my faith kept me at peace.

> *You will guard him and keep him in perfect and constant peace whose mind [both its inclination and its character] is stayed on You, because he commits himself to You, leans on You, and hopes confidently in You.*
> *Isaiah 26:3 AMP*

DON'T GET CAUGHT UNPREPARED

Sometimes people do not believe me when I share with them how I handled everything. I can tell they do not believe, because they will keep asking the same questions over and over again, like "How did you *really* feel?" Spiritually, I was prepared for this process, even though I had no past experiences like this as a basis. In the natural I would have never imagined that I could prepare for this in any way. Building up our faith muscles beforehand is how we prepare ourselves for the hard times that are ahead. We will address building up your faith more in the coming chapters, but know that nothing catches God by surprise and He does not intend to have it catch us off guard either. God is always preparing us for everything we go through. We just may not realize it at the time. For instance, Pastor Mike's last lesson at church before we entered into this challenge was on how we hear better with our spiritual ears, as opposed to with our natural ears. That lesson was key for me when I was going through this, and allowed me to quickly tap into my spiritual senses versus responding to what was going on in the natural with my physical senses. At first, I thought I was sucker punched, but when I looked back I realized that God was preparing me the whole time. I guarantee you that when you look back on your lessons, you will be able to see how God made provision in preparing you. A scripture that my husband always stressed was Proverbs 3:6, *'In all your ways acknowledge Him, And He shall direct your paths.'* God is waiting for us to allow Him to lead. Our faith opens the doorway for Him to work wonders in our lives. Everything I did was led by the Lord, including Operation Faith!

FAITH PRINCIPLE FOUR

Initiate An Operation Faith.

Get out of "faithless" environments while you are in a faith process. Document and remind yourself of the positive milestones. I used video, but you may want to journal or photograph… The key is to constantly remind yourself how great God is, versus how big your problem is.

Take a quick mental survey of the people and the environments that you subject yourself to. Are there people who need to be removed or places that you need to remove yourself from? Include your physical, spiritual and mental environments. Faith comes by hearing, so be sure the words you're depositing into your brain contribute to your Operation Faith.

WORD WEAPON

"For we walk by faith, not by sight."

2 Corinthians 5:7

FIVE
BELIEVERS BELIEVE

People are quick to recite the verse, "for without faith it is impossible to please God", but then the question is, why are so many of us operating in fear and doubt? And if "faith without works is dead," then why are we not collectively seeing the living result of faith in our lives? As a believer, I want to remind you that we demonstrate our faith by *displaying* it visibly. Can people see your faith in action? If the answer is no, chances are, your faith is not where it should be in order for you to withstand any process that you are facing. When you are faced with a challenge, if you are walking by faith, you should have a level of peace on the inside of you that sustains you because your faith has already dictated the end. Like Abraham, you are convinced! You cannot display a "woe is me" disposition every time something happens to you, and convince me that you are living by faith. Yes, you may feel sucker punched briefly, but then you remember that you are a believer! Your spirit man begins to echo the words of Jesus when He said,

> *"Father, I thank you that you heard me. I know that you always hear me,"*
> John 11:41,42 NCV

God ALWAYS responds to faith. He does not reward pity parties. Sometimes I wish He did because I would not have gone through some of the dumb stuff I went through for so long. As a believer you have an advantage over everyone else, because we are spirit led. Jesus went away but sent The Helper, Holy Spirit, to help us. The Father carefully orchestrated our steps before He put us in the earth. You do not have to be ignorant of the strategies of your enemy! Your job is simply to believe that the Father has you covered. It is amazing that people have been given the will and authority to believe whatever they want and most still choose to believe the wrong thing. For instance, you have two choices-the first being to believe you will live if you have cancer and the second to believe that you will die because you have cancer. Most choose to believe the latter. Whether we choose to believe or not, that choice will set our destiny. I know that this is not easy for everyone, but it can be. Each person, depending on the environment they have been subjected to, may have a different level of faith. Some people have various complexes, inner belief systems, and even trust issues that prevent them from living solely by faith. Fear also cripples some people into unbelief. My mother has always been terrified about the big "C." It was so bad, that she would never even utter the word "cancer". Her father died from cancer, and she always thought that if someone had cancer and the doctors opened that person up, air would get to the cancer, and it would spread, and as a result, she would die. Of course this was very superstitious, but it was a real fear for her. The day she came home and told us she was diagnosed cancer, it was rough. Not because I did not believe God could heal her, but I knew how afraid she was. My fear was that her fear would kill her instead of the cancer. Thank God she found out it was only in stage one. So she had to go through two weeks of radiation everyday, and now she is cancer free!

Inner belief systems and trust issues can absolutely play a role in our ability to operate in faith. I say this because we all are products of the environment that we come from. It does matter what church you go to and whom you set yourself to learn from. Everything in the spiritual can be compared to the natural. For instance, if you did not trust your father, it may be challenging for you to trust God, your heavenly Father. Developing faith is a conditioning process; much like an athlete or new military recruit goes through prior to playing in their first professional game or fighting in their first serious battle. During basic training, a new recruit does not focus on those weeks of physical and mental tests. He instead focuses on the end reward of completing a major step in his career, and being in a position to serve his country. While you are in a process, this should be your same approach. Your position should be to believe, and see the end. As such is our God. He sees the end from the beginning.

[God is there standing at] the very beginning telling you what the ending will be, All along letting you in on what is going to happen, Assuring you, "I'm in this for the long haul, I'll do exactly what I set out to do,'
Isaiah 46:10 MSG

If you can stay focused on the promise during your process, operating in faith and getting through the challenge will become much easier.

THE ONE NON-NEGOTIABLE

I know how hard it can be when you are dealing with things in the natural arena. I have been there when my marriage was terrible. I did not want to pray. I did not want to believe God for restoration, but eventually I knew that because I wanted my marriage to work I had to start applying the Word. If you are not built up in the Word, it will not be easy to pray for the outcome you want from God, especially when things seem destined for the worst. Your flesh wants to do things a certain way, and demonstrating faith may be a bit uncomfortable at times. You may even feel silly believing for things that you cannot see. However, believing in the unseen must become your one non-negotiable. Seeing the unseen is faith. I am not telling you that you have to always keep a smile on your face, and I am not telling you it will always be easy to stand. But as you grow stronger spiritually, you will find that "faithing it" will become easier until you actually do "make it."

If those that are called to the righteousness of God are required to live by faith, and we are they, then living by faith should be the one behavior that you do not forsake. Unfortunately, so many Christians do not know and understand how faith works, or know that they have enough faith right now to do life successfully. Romans 12:3 says that God has given to every man the measure of faith. With this lack of understanding of the faith each of us contains, many Christians never see God's abundant plan for their lives play out. This, to me, is the ultimate tragedy-people with an insurmountable amount of potential that they simply cannot manifest because they do not know how to operate and exercise their faith. My prayer for you is that you would avoid this misfortune at all costs. I want you, instead, to think about faith as the magnet to attract your future. When you operate in faith you tap into Jesus' resurrection power to raise every dead situation in your life.

In Matthew chapter 8, we meet a Roman officer, who had great faith. When Jesus entered the town of Capernaum, the officer came to Him pleading, *"Lord, my servant is lying at home paralyzed dreadfully tormented."* Jesus was ready to go and heal him. He even told the officer, *"I will come and heal him."* But the officer said, *"I am not worthy that you should come under my roof, but only speak a word, and my servant will be healed."* Now just wait one minute! The surety of this man's faith was mind-blowing to say the least. Could you imagine Jesus offering to come to your home to do some hands-on healing? I'm not sure about you, but I would most likely take Him up on that offer! But no, that Roman officer just asked Jesus to speak a word. That great act of faith impressed Jesus. The Bible says that Jesus, *"Marveled, and said to everyone else who was around, "I have not found such great faith, not even in Israel..."* To be a believer whose faith has God marveled, now that is awesome! Your faith moves God!

> *It's impossible to please God apart from faith. And why? Because anyone who wants to approach God must believe both that he exists and that he cares enough to respond to those who seek him.*
> *Hebrews 11:6 MSG*

Faith is like a magnet that attracts the manifested power of God to your life and ultimately your situation. You must start to believe that God cares enough to respond, and has already given you the power to resurrect every area of your life; that includes your mind, relationships, finances… whatever your thing is. No matter what process you are in right now just know that the manifestation of what you are believing for will show itself in response to your faith.

UNCHANGING FAITH CYCLE

God has given each of us various assignments to fulfill throughout our lives. The difficulties that we endure can be used to prepare us for the next assignment. The process only serves as opportunity to build our character and flex our faith muscles. The Word of God says, *'...but we glory in tribulations also, knowing that tribulation worketh patience; and patience, experience, and experience, hope: and hope maketh not ashamed'* Romans 5:3-5. What you are going through and what you have been through may have been intended to break you in the eyes of your enemy, but you are strong enough to handle the process. The faith cycle of believing God through a process, seeing His promises manifest and leaving with a testimony has not changed in over 2,000 years since Jesus walked the earth. Just read the gospels of Matthew, Mark, Luke and John. Despite each gospel being written from a different perspective, you will notice that each book stresses how people were healed when they believed. This is so embedded in my heart, I can hear Jesus saying, "Your faith has made you whole," to everyone whose faith He encountered. Afterwards, He instructed those who were once sick to go forth and spread the good news about what God had done. The faith cycle is to speak, believe, receive— and then go and testify. This, just like the cycle of life and death, is one that you cannot escape. If you try to escape this process, you will fall short of reaching your desired end. The test, the trial, and the fight are always the tough part. Dropping out of a process is a demonstration of your lack of faith, and it is why so many people will never experience God's promises for them. Your faith, or lack thereof, dictates what happens next. Many people start off in faith, but as their process continues and time passes, they get out of the faith cycle, and fall victim to the process. When the process takes too long and they are too impatient to wait, they cannot see the manifestations of what they believe for so they get tired and quit. Make a decision today that you will *quit being a quitter*.

DEMONSTRATED FAITH

While my husband was in the hospital, people were affected by our faith. Because we demonstrated that we are believers, the staff knew our family was different. Perhaps the most effective way we demonstrated our faith was by the words that we spoke over Mike, allowing them to hear so they could witness the power of God. I told you that Joshua was not always 100% confident that his dad would make it through. Still, he refused to speak those words. My kids have been taught that the power of their words can produce life or death according to the Word of God. Scripture teaches us to take no thought by *saying*. You can think all you want but do not open your mouth with something negative. We spoke words of life, and our actions and attitudes fell in line with our words. Eventually the doctors and nurses began to speak our faith language too. Writing this has me excited all over again. I thank

God for His saving power! They stopped making statements like, "If he makes it," or "If this works…" No matter how the situation looked, they would say, "When this procedure works…" The word "if" has doubt embedded within it, while "when" is rooted in faith and assurance. We prayed for, and with the staff. We demonstrated our faith by ministering to them and other patients constantly. We sang worship songs in the waiting room and prayed over my husband, as he lay there unconscious. I put headphones on him, so he would not hear all of the sounds of the machines and the beeps. I was determined to pump his spirit man with scriptures and lessons on healing all day. Dr. Smith suggested that at night, before I left, I play music and treat him like he was aware of what was going on. This would allow him to know the shift from day to night by the different playlists. I did not know if he could hear or was aware of it, but I did not care. I was willing to do whatever was necessary to demonstrate my faith. The hospital staff, after a while, started to check his phone to make sure the playlist was still playing. They practically became a part of our family. We laughed together, and shared serious moments, joys, stresses and celebrations. This sharing even included their struggles and private lives. Showing and proving your faith is not just about trusting God, but it is about caring for and serving others.

    This is exactly the scenario that plays out in Mark chapter 9 (also told in Matthew 17:14 and Luke 9:37-42). I am going to paraphrase the writers of the Gospel. There was a boy who suffered with severe epilepsy. It was so bad that he often fell into fire and water. The disciples tried to heal the boy, but were unable to do so. They later asked Jesus why, and he told them, *"Because of your unbelief..."* But of course, Jesus healed the epileptic boy. In Mark 9:23, Jesus told the boy's dad, "If you can believe, all things are possible to him who believes." The Bible says that, *"Immediately the father of the child cried out and said with tears, 'Lord, I believe; [BUT] help my unbelief!'"* He was willing to believe what the Lord had told him and positioned himself in faith, asking Jesus for help along the way. And even though he knew doubt had the potential to rise up, he obeyed God and focused on believing that which was promised.

Always operate in faith and ask Holy Spirit, The Helper, to pick up the slack where your faith lacks. You have every tool you need to stand at the end of this having obtained victory. Be a believer that believes.

FAITH PRINCIPLE FIVE

Show your faith.

Your faith is a magnet for the positive blessings you want to see. Your faith is a magnet for Jesus' saving power to be activated. Your faith is a magnet to bring others closer to God. Even when having faith seems silly, pointless or challenging, 'faith it' until you really feel that way. Holy Spirit is in you. After you have shown, and grown your faith—prove it. Become a promise magnet.

Each process is essential to your growth as a believer, and developing your faith is a key part of being able to stand strong in any process (the spiritual fruit of long suffering). Begin to keep track of your faith battles in a journal. Note what you are trusting and believing God for, how you are showing your faith, and the things that happen during your process. You want to remind yourself that if He did it before, He can and will do it again.

WORD WEAPON

"Count it all joy, my brothers, when you meet trials of various kinds, for you know that the testing of your faith produces steadfastness. And let steadfastness have its full effect, that you may be perfect and complete, lacking in nothing."

James 1:2-4

SIX
THE WAITING ROOM

We took over the waiting room, which held about twenty people. There was a coffee table of old magazines that no one seemed interested in reading, and an old TV that played soap operas around the clock. The room was dull and drab, with light blue walls and soiled, mismatched chairs. To make matters worse, there were no windows because it was in the middle of the hospital. You could tell this room was not built for long-term stay, but the condition of the room did not faze me. I escaped by meditating on another picture. I knew I had to make some changes to make this space more accommodating for myself and other visitors. So I would get there early in the morning and set up shop. I took over the room and when people came in that were not apart of my family, they knew they had entered into my space. Others in my family would trickle in throughout the day to keep me company. My sister Darnice was my sidekick, right there by my side day in and day out. I thank God daily for her. She made sure I was always taken care of, along with the Smiths. My brother-in-law Dwight would bring a cooler full of sodas and junk food, like we were at a cookout. I was in school getting my master's degree in Human Services when Mike got sick, so I had to do my homework while I waited. I would bring my books, study, and write papers right there in the waiting room. People asked me if it was hard to focus. Yes, but not because my husband was in an induced coma. It was hard for me to focus because I was busy ministering to everyone that came in the room.

  Many translate Isaiah 40:31 differently because of the word "wait." It reads, *"But those who wait on the Lord shall renew their strength..."* There are many definitions to the word wait and I choose to believe that this does not mean to sit around and do nothing. When I think of the word "wait" I often think of a waitress, waiting or serving tables. This reminds me that waiting is not merely about a pause in time-it is about serving. So while I am in any process I take my attention off of my own situation and I serve others. This is exactly what I did while I sat in the waiting room. Do you get it? "Waiting room." I served others that came in with whatever I could. I bought lunch, made coffee, passed out tissue, gave an ear and prayed; but most of all, I led people to Jesus. The dispositions of people that were coming in for their loved ones were very disheartening to see. I met mothers, fathers, daughters, sons, and friends of patients and many were hopeless. Remember, this was the ICU waiting area where not much hope was given, so if you did not come in with it, do not expect to get it after you have arrived. One young man was there before Mike arrived, and was there long after Mike got there, but he was not in ICU. He was in a regular room. He would come to the waiting room, where we were, to get coffee and sugar packs for his food. I ministered to him every chance I had. When it was time for him to leave the hospital, he only had shorts and a tee shirt to wear home. Well, it was hot when he arrived in the hospital back in July, but by this time, the seasons had changed, and it was cold when he left. He lived hours away, so he was taking a Greyhound Bus home. You know I could not allow him to travel in those clothes. So I sent my sister to buy him something new to wear from the gift shop.

GOD IS IN YOUR TOMORROW TODAY

One day I was sitting there next to Mike's bed, and as I looked around at everything that was going on, I heard God's voice say to me, "DeeDee, I want you to focus on the promise and not the process."

Puzzled, I responded, "God, that is what I'm doing. I am not worried. I am not going through anything. You know I am not looking at this stuff." At that time Mike's numbers were going up and down, his heart was unstable, and his kidneys appeared to be shutting down.

So, I said, "God, what is this about? You know I am okay. Why are You telling me this? What do You see that I do not see?" That is when Holy Spirit led me to read Mark chapter 5. This chapter talks about the woman with the issue of blood, but as I read I was reminded that the story did not start with the woman with the issue of blood. If you read back a little further, you will see that Jesus walked through the crowds with intentions to go take care of Jairus's need. Jairus saw Jesus coming, stopped him and said, "Look my daughter is sick and laying at the point of death. Can you go and pray for her?" As you know, Jesus is moved by faith. Jairus was bold enough to step to Jesus and say, "Can you come to my house?" So Jesus was on His way to Jairus' house, but then He ran into *this chick* with an issue. After grabbing ahold of His hem, and being healed, Jesus begins to talk with her. The Bible says that she began to tell Jesus her *whole* story. Now as you can imagine, this is the last thing that Jairus wanted to see. Jairus was focused on his daughter. He wanted to make sure she would live. He did not want to see her die because of some interference that was about to happen. So here

Jesus is, standing there talking to the woman with the issue of blood. And it says that people from Jairus' house came to him and told him not to trouble the Master any longer, because his daughter was dead. I love what Jesus did after that. The Bible says that as soon as Jesus heard what the people told Jairus, He looked at Jairus and said, "Don't be afraid." He said, "Only believe." So after my moment with God in the hospital, I read this, and said, *"That's it!"* I had an epiphany. *Jesus was already in my tomorrow, that day*. He was not only re-assuring me of the outcome, but He was allowing me to see the testimony that would come from this process. In the book of Mark, Jesus knew that if doubt and unbelief had penetrated Jairus' heart, his daughter would have never been raised from the dead.

This is why when you are going through a challenge or dealing with a situation, and when the enemy comes to tell you that you are about to go under, you have got to say, "No, I bind that in the name of Jesus." Do not allow garbage from the enemy to penetrate your heart.

MINISTER THROUGH THE MESS

It had been three weeks since my husband was in the hospital. I missed church every weekend because I was at the hospital. As a pastor's wife, being away from your church that long is almost unheard of. As I mentioned, Pastor Mike had always been a private guy when it came to his health. I knew that people would find out that he was in the hospital, and I eventually started seeing people in the waiting room that wanted to know why I was there. I kept his illness a secret for a couple of weeks or so as I was still trying to process this whole thing. I just needed time to get concrete information about how he was doing and if he would be gone for a long while. The week he went in the hospital, was also the week we were supposed to be on vacation. That week was fine, as far as church was concerned, but the next Sunday we had friends and family day scheduled at church. I had to say something because people were going to ask, "Where is Pastor Mike?" So I began to strategize again.

    I decided to record a video and I sent it to the church. I began by saying, "I know some of you are wondering where Pastor Mike is …" I proceeded to tell them he was ill, in the hospital, and that he would be fine. At this point, I was truly prophesying over his health, because in the natural, he was completely unconscious. Two weeks after sending the first video, I went to church and ministered. I remember being so excited to give them this Word God gave me. Brittney and I were sitting in the hospital cafeteria and I started to share what God told me. He said, "Focus on the promise and not the process." I was so hyped that I stood up in the middle of the hospital cafeteria talking to her and said,

"That is my message that I have to teach our church!" She was laughing at me and wanted me to calm down but I could not compose myself. During that ride to church on September 13, 2014, I could not contain myself. I prepared to minister knowing God had given me that Word! In the middle of my message I heard, "Your name is Dr. PP." I thought to myself, "No, my name is Dr. DeeDee," but Holy Spirit said, "No it's Dr. PP, because you are 'pissed' and 'pumped'." Now I know a lot of people do not like that word because of its negative connotation. However, in that moment, that was the perfect way to describe where I was. I was indeed pissed off that the devil put his hands on my man, but I was pumped because I know I was equipped for the fight. See, the devil cannot have ANYTHING that belongs to me — not one pencil or piece of paper! He comes to kill, steal and destroy, but we have the power to overcome his tactics because the Greater One lives on the inside of us. While my husband was still in ICU, I ministered the Word of God with all boldness and authority, because I knew God had us. I was sure of the outcome. Most people would not have dared to get up and share the Word I shared because they would have been reluctant to put themselves out there, thinking, "What if this thing does not turn out the way I am saying it will?" I was way past that point. That was not my concern.

One week following that sermon, I sent another video, and I told them, "Okay, come to church, because I am going to tell you what is going on with Pastor. Tell your nosey neighbor and your best friend to be at church next week." This was after Mike was stabilized. The following Sunday, every service was packed. When I preached, again Holy Spirit led, as I updated our congregation on the state of our pastor. I preached about focusing on God's promise, not the process. The church received the message well, and ultimately, everything we did during this time contributed to a significant growth in our ministry. Many times, people can get goofy when the leader is not in place like usual, but that did not happen in our church. My brother-in-law, Pastor Dewayne, led the ministers and oversaw the ministry as a whole, keeping everyone on point to continue to do what they have been taught. Throughout the time when Pastor Mike was out, we did not have the any issues that may be expected when their leader is away. Everyone continued business as usual, in a *spirit of faith*, operating the same way our Pastor had taught us prior to his hospitalization.

WAITING SONG

While you are waiting during the process, it is important to keep things moving along. Again, and I stress this time, if you have faith in God's promises, your whole world should not be shaken up and destroyed when you are going through a storm. Make your waiting room a productive space of praise and worship that gives glory to God. Praise and worship became my abode. In Psalms 32:7 David said, *"You are a hiding place for me; You, Lord, preserve me from trouble, You surround me with songs and shouts of deliverance."* God was doing just that for me as I intentionally sought His presence as my refuge.

He has given me a new song to sing, a hymn of praise to our God. Many will see what he has done and be astounded. They will put their trust in the LORD.
Psalms 40:3 NLT

Just as God gave David a new song to sing, He *literally* gave me one too! I wrote a song while I was in the waiting room. It was funny how it happened. I was talking to my family, telling them that I did not know how anyone could go through what I was going through without Jesus. I began to sing, "I wouldn't want to do life without YOU." I made everyone in the room sing it with me while I recorded them. Then I sent a few lines and a melody to Tim Bowman, Jr., a gospel recording artist, who is now my son-in-law, and asked him to fix it up for me. He took those few lines, and created an awesome song. Once I heard the song, I got really excited and went to the church and told everyone that they would soon hear my "waiting room" song. Tim sang the song at church one Sunday, while Mike was still in the hospital, and it took on a life of its own. I had no idea how far it would go! He was simply doing me a favor for an "in-house deal." To our surprise, someone from a radio station heard about the song and called the church. The local gospel station wanted a copy to play on-air. But that was a no-no, because Tim is signed to a label and was not allowed to produce music outside of that contract. I totally understood that prior to asking him to work on it for me. Again, it was supposed to be a song for our church. Well, when the church did not send the song, the extremely persistent station called his label. They *really* wanted to get that song on air. Tim had some explaining to do once the record execs learned he had produced a song outside of his contract, so he sent the song to his label. But after his team at the label heard the song, and the story behind it, they loved it too! It eventually ended up on his album. By the way, that album, entitled *Listen*, hit number one on the Billboard charts the first week it was released.

    Well, I do not know if you know this, but writers get royalties once a song is published, played and sold. Okay, follow me down this spiritual road. You will certainly like this one — the Bible says in Proverbs 6:31 that the thief, when he is caught, has to pay you back seven times over. That sucker took almost a year from me! During this process, I could not enjoy my husband like I should have been able to. I missed his touch. I missed his kiss. I missed his conversation. I missed getting in the car and going wherever we wanted to go. I missed my vacation that we were supposed to have gone on. I felt like I had been robbed of the joys of our bond for months, and I wanted the one that took it to pay me back! So the thief owes me, and I am going to make him pay for every day, every minute, and every second that he stole. Why not start with paying on a song birthed out of my worship? I am not backing down or giving up on God's promises, and neither should you. You are also entitled to some stuff that the enemy stole from you. Do not allow him to keep anything that is yours. Go get your royalties!

FAITH PRINCIPLE SIX

Wait with purpose.

The key to waiting is waiting with purpose, while you remain focused on God's promise. Do not sit idly by watching the time pass as you are going through the process. If I can share anything about the art of waiting, I would say to follow my lead—worship, pray, minister to yourself and others, empower yourself and fellowship with the circle of soldiers who are fighting this battle with you.

Now, I want you to start rethinking your "Waiting Room." As you are waiting for God's promises for you to come to pass, are you waiting with intention and expectation or are you waiting idly? Are you worshiping God for not leaving you, ministering to yourself and others, praying your way through and doing things to empower yourself? Is your focus during this process on God and what He is doing for you? Wait with purpose.

WORD WEAPON

"But those who wait on the Lord. Shall renew their strength; they shall mount up with wings like eagles, they shall run and not be weary, they shall walk and not faint."

Isaiah 40:31

SEVEN
FAITH CREDENTIALS

Truthfully speaking, although I remained positive, I was pissed at the devil for touching something that belongs to me. My stance was, "How dare you devil?" I was angry with the enemy; and I used that anger as fuel to stretch my faith and remain steadfast. Believers, do not back down when the enemy attacks! You must remember that he has no right to anything that belongs to you. God has given you the right to say, "I am not going to take this," and the power to do something about it!

Years ago, the devil tried to take my only son, Josh—my baby. It hurt like hell, but I went into full-fledge fight mode and fought that sucker with every ounce of faith I had! Josh was sixteen at the time. My husband and I were lying in the bed. It was getting pretty late, and Mike asked me if I had heard from our son. Up until that point, I had not even thought about the fact that he was not home. The phone rang at midnight, and it was the sheriff saying that they had arrested my son. He had been charged with attempted murder. You can only imagine how I felt - mama's baby boy, the pastor's son was locked up for attempted murder. To get a call like that…it felt like my heart dropped to the floor. This situation was painful. I believe going through that situation helped to build me up for future faith fights. Josh had violated one of our rules - he had a person in the car that he did not know. He was somewhere and a fight broke out. When they were pulling off, the guy he did not know took a gun and shot into the air. Josh thought someone was shooting at them, so he took off—speeding away from the scene. When the other guy said he was shooting, Josh realized and put him out of the car. My son drove away in his own car, and later went to turn himself in. They locked him up, and charged him with attempted murder. $80,000 later, they realized that my son did not know this boy who had the gun. Even the mother (whose house the fight was at) knew Josh, and eventually she and other witnesses came forward on his behalf and said it was not him. They called it *nolle prosequi*, which means null process. In other words, they dropped all the charges. Although that situation was agonizing and costly, I did not give up; I refused to let the enemy win.

As long as I was involved, the devil was not going to have the last word in Mike's situation either. And I was most definitely involved. I knew my husband's work was not over. While Mike was in the hospital I had a lot of time to reflect on prior conversations. I thought about how we would sit and discuss who would die first. This may seem strange to some, but we often discuss topics others refuse to touch. It started years ago when we sat down with an estate lawyer and he gave us a bunch of scenarios on who and how one of us would die. I remember the discussion like it was yesterday. The lawyer asked Mike if he were to die first, would he still want me to get his money if I remarried. Mike's eyes stretched as wide as mine. I have large eyes and I did not know that his could become as large as mine, until he was presented with the thought of me marrying someone else! I know, funny right? Immediately he said that I was not going to get a dime if I remarried! Then, all of a sudden, he seemed to have an epiphany. He said, "Oh, she will die before me because she would not be any good if I died first." From that moment forward this became our inside joke. Remembering those words that he had been saying to me for years is what I held on to while he was in the worst condition ever. The thought of him dying was never an option for me. I started to remind him of those playful but meaningful words. I would get in his ear and say, "You remember our agreement that I would go first."

I also meditated on him standing and preaching in Faith City. Faith City is the next phase of his vision for our ministry. God would not give him a vision to fulfill and not keep him around to complete it. There were too many unfulfilled prophecies. I know a lot of people die before fulfilling purpose, but my husband does not just talk the talk, he walks the walk. He walks into everything he talks about. This in mind, I declared that he would live and not die so he could carry out his assignment. Twenty years ago my big brother Rick ministered to me, saying that I was an incubator to Mike's vision. This truly resonated as everyone that knows me knows that I hold fast to the words that Mike speaks. I take what he says and I nurture it until it comes to pass. I pray over his vision and there are times when I remind him, "Baby you said…". Since this has been my custom, it was easy to remind myself of what he's told me even while he was lying there unaware of his surroundings. I continued to see Mike rising out of that hospital bed, healthy and whole; preaching the gospel. I also began to envision us vacationing, being in that hospital for quite some time I could have used a beach. I remained committed to this faith fight. As you go through your process and train your faith, you—just as I did— will realize just how much fight you have in you, and that taking the enemy's attack with no rebuttal is out of the question!

I need you to get this ingrained in your mind — everything in life happens through a process. As Solomon says in Ecclesiastes, "To everything there is a season, a time for every purpose under heaven". If you know now that the process is inevitable, you should always prepare. During this time, I realized that I was already prepared for what I was facing because of years of training my faith. Prior to starting our church, Mike and I would sit by ourselves and have Bible study. Since he was so wise in the Word, I wanted to know the Bible the way he did. Mike would literally sit and teach me all he knew, and show me how to see things in the Word that I had not noticed before. I was like a sponge during those times. Those moments were really special to me as I grew to know and love Mike as a leader, teacher, and most importantly, as my pastor. I learned the various promises of the Bible that I was entitled to, and learning those promises strengthened my faith.

The Bible explains that God gives each of us a measure of faith and grace (Rom. 12:3), and that we grow our faith by hearing the Word of God (Rom. 10:17). I believed that God would raise my husband from his deathbed, because of prior experiences that strengthened my faith. By activating my faith, I put the Word of God into practice. This is an important point because many people will try to do exactly what I did, and expect to receive the same results, but without having the same faith. I am writing this book not only to tell you what I did, but to teach you the faith principles that helped me get the results that I maintain today. You cannot compare testimonies. You have to compare faith; if you are comparing anything at all. Prior to this process, not only had I relied on God to do the impossible and stood confident in my faith, so had my husband.

Some of my personal faith fights were also concerning my own health. About 15 years ago, I started to experience excruciating pain whenever I walked - I could not barely walk in my shoes without feeling discomfort. The doctors told me I had rheumatoid arthritis. Maybe you or someone you know has dealt with the agonizing pain of arthritis; if so, you know what I mean when I tell you I did not want to live my life like this. The thought of not wearing my heels was too much for me! Apostle Price laid hands on me and prayed that I would receive healing from this illness. Meanwhile, I did not sit around feeling sorry for myself. I had no time to waste. I simply used the angry energy as motivation to exercise. I came home and put on my tennis shoes and walked around my driveway meditating and declaring, "by His stripes I am healed". I took the power and authority that God gave me and used it. I believed and received, even when my body was not manifesting what I was believing. Eventually the pain subsided. Although that was many years ago, sometimes when I feel my feet starting to hurt, I begin to thank God again for my continued triumph over that illness. I am not claiming nor will I ever accept arthritis for my life! I have since been completely healed from arthritis and now strut in my six-inch heels effortlessly.

At another point, I was diagnosed with a hyperactive thyroid. It was not healthy for me, but I did not mind it at all at first because it caused me to lose weight as opposed to gaining. What woman would not want that problem? Nonetheless I knew it was not healthy so I went to the doctor's office, there he gave me three choices: 1. To have the thyroid removed with surgery, and take a pill for the rest of my life; 2. To have radiation, and take a pill for the rest of my life; or 3. Just take a pill for the rest of my life. Well, I do not like taking pills! As you can see consuming pills was required regardless of which option I would have selected. I have tried to take daily vitamins, and I have never been successful. I always forget. With that said, I knew I could not commit to taking pills everyday forever, and furthermore I did not want to! So I considered the cost of owning this problem and thought to myself, "Okay you want me to take a pill for the rest of my life—something that I do not like to do, and something that I cannot even remember to do half the time?" At that point I started talking to God and trusting Him to remove that issue from my body. I meditated on the promises of healing that I am entitled to in the Word of God. I took those pills for about two weeks, and then I stopped. Two weeks after I stopped taking the pills, I went back to the doctor, and he told me, "Just keep doing what you are doing. Everything is looking good!" Well, I knew I had stopped taking the pills, but I did not tell him that. I just thought to myself, "Okay great, God is working it out." Eventually, I obtained victory over that issue and was healed. Fifteen years later, I do not have to take pills for thyroid problems.

> *Therefore, since we are surrounded by such a huge crowd of witnesses to the life of faith, let us strip off every weight that slows us down, especially the sin that so easily hinders our progress. And let us run with endurance the race that God has set before us.*
> Hebrews 12:1 NLT

I am not alone in participating and obtaining victory in my faith fights! We have a crowd of witnesses in the Word of God, and believers around you who are exercising their faith and shutting the enemy down. Hebrews chapter 11 lists what is commonly referred to as the Hall of

Faith-biblical characters that championed testimonies of tremendous faith. The list includes characters such as Noah, who by faith prepared an ark for the saving of his household; Abraham, who by faith offered up his son Isaac to be a sacrifice; Moses, who by faith chose to be with the people of God rather than enjoying the passing pleasures of sin in Egypt. I have added my name to the list, and you should do the same. Go ahead and say out loud, "By faith, I, [insert your name], ...". Now complete that declaration by shouting the promise you are believing God for!

Be prepared for the pending processes by building your faith NOW. Start trusting and believing God for what you want and need. Set yourself up to win your next process by making deposits into your faith account TODAY. At the end of this chapter, you will find several verses related to faith to help get you started.

The faith that I had deposited into my faith bank up until that point allowed me to hear the voice of God, and understand what to do during the process. I knew that this process would be Mike's testimony, and so I documented every step of the way to show what God would do for those who believed. I believed. I want you to experience the resurrection power of Jesus Christ in your life, and I want you to know, just like I know, that God keeps His promises. *Stay in faith!*

FAITH PRINCIPLE SEVEN

Stand on God's Word.

Stand on the word of God, and the proof of Jesus' resurrection power to strengthen your faith. Make deposits daily into your Faith Account, because you will need to withdraw when you encounter the next process. Remember that as long as the earth remains, there will be seedtime and harvest. You will enter process after process in route to your promises from God. Prepare yourself through faith.

The verses that follow will help you apply God's word to your life, and give you practical teachings about faith. Refer to them, circle them, and pull them out of this book if you need to. Attach these verses to your fridge, bathroom mirror or car dashboard. Just make sure they are attached to your heart so that you can live by faith.

It's time for The Promise!

WORDS OF FAITH

And whatever things you ask in prayer, believing, you will receive Matthew 21:22

For with God nothing will be impossible.
Luke 1:37

That your faith should not be in the wisdom of men but in the power of God.
1 Corinthians 2:5

"Be still, and know that I am God…"
Psalm 46:10

I have fought the good fight, I have finished the race, I have kept the faith.
2 Timothy 4:7

Jesus said to him, "If you can believe, all things are possible to him who believes."
Mark 9:23

Commit your way to the Lord, Trust also in Him,
And He shall bring it to pass. He shall bring forth your righteousness as the light,
And your justice as the noonday.
Psalm 37:5-6

PART II
THE PROMISE

EIGHT
TRANSITION

I have to begin this chapter with a praise break! I remember the first words my husband spoke, and yes, I recorded them. After weeks of being unable to communicate, he uttered, "Thank you Jesus!" I believe this was the first time I cried. It had been a long time since I heard his voice. Then I made him tell me that he loved me, and yes - I cried again. These were happy tears for sure. Everyone in the room was ecstatic to hear him! The devil thought he had silenced my husband forever, but not so. The man that was down was now back up. A couple of weeks later he started telling me what to do so I knew he was doing great then. I had to relinquish my control because while he was down I was making all of the decisions. I was ready to give that responsibility back. Before, I was the one making all of the videos to update the partners at church, but when he was able to sit up I had him make his own video. At the time he still did not have his permanent valve to give him sound so he could not speak. We wrote the message he wanted to share on cards and flipped the cards for him because he was unable to move his arms. One of his cards read, "The devil tried to kill your boy." With this I want to encourage you. Do not allow the devil to kill your dreams or desires. Fight for what you want!

Often the transition from a difficult "process" to the joy-filled "promise" can seem like a long time, while other transitions seem to happen overnight. No matter how fast or slow a transition seems, it is important to realize that in the spirit realm, God has already worked in ways that we could not see—for longer than we know. I have come to learn that for God there are no emergencies and our faith is what makes things happen on earth. Time holds no barriers or hindrances for what our faith is able to do. Mike's "miracle" comeback is an example of this. God is not constrained by the natural limits of time. Something that takes five years to do, God can do in five minutes. But when we lack faith, we place God in a box and hinder Him from doing what we need Him to do for us.

Mike was on the ECMO machine from August 22 to September 9, 2014. He was still in ICU at Washington Hospital Center at that time, and it was indeed a medical miracle that my husband survived. Few people survive after having an oxygen level of 22% being unconscious, and in critical condition. The medical staff originally told us that after Mike left ICU he would be transferred to a regular hospital room. But after three weeks on the ECMO machine, followed by thirteen days of treatment in ICU, Mike was doing so well that he skipped the step-down room and transitioned directly to a rehabilitation center in Laurel, Maryland. Nobody does that! Most people go from ICU to a standard hospital room, and then to a rehab facility; but Mike's recovery was far from standard.

  When Mike woke up, he had a ton of questions about what had been going on, and wanted an update on everything. I remember that day like it was yesterday. I entered his room the same as I had every other day, and he asked why was he in the hospital. I thought it best that I spoon feed him details. For one, he was still high on all of the drugs and would not have remembered, so I just gave him pieces. What really shocked me was when he told me the exact number of weeks he was out of church. He really loves the members that God has assigned to him. They sent him a lot of cards while he was in rehab. They tell me that when the video played at church, the partners went crazy, cheering and crying and slapping hands in celebration. They were finally able to see their pastor after months of his absence and knew that God had answered their prayers. This let me know that we were truly all in this together. He left the hospital on September 22, 2014. His rapid recovery went right in line with what we were praying for from Amos 9:13 in the Message Bible—*blessings and healing happening so fast 'that your head would swim.'* This scripture had manifested in Mike's life. He had experienced a supernatural healing that could have only been explained as a work of God. This transition happened very quickly, even by natural timing. One minute he was barely able to breathe on his own, and the next, he was going into rehab, skipping the normal "process" that the hospital expected. Do not ever let anyone tell you that specific, strategic and simultaneous prayers by soldiers of God won't work!

When Mike first arrived to Laurel Regional Hospital on September 22, he could only move his neck, and he was still on an oxygen machine and unable to breathe on his own. During that time, I celebrated every milestone. I documented and recorded everything from the first time he held his head up to the first time he lifted his arm. It was all a part of the plan and boosted the confidence of others with his miraculous progress. He started intense treatment, seven days a week. His treatment plan perplexed the medical staff. They were not used to having patients go through physical therapy everyday. On September 29, after a week in rehab, they gave him a valve to speak. Despite his objections, he was also given a feeding tube. Yet his attitude was encouraging. The hospital staff grew to love him, because he was so determined. And as I sat in that room with him, I could not help but to be in good spirits as well. A month prior, this ordeal had threatened to take him out, and I knew that it had been our faith that brought us through. Rehab was certainly better than ICU, so we had no complaints. We were indeed blessed, and the promise was closer in sight than it had been since he first became ill. However, we weren't in the clear yet.

The treatment was very challenging for us—both physically and mentally. I stayed in Mike's room most of the time, and helped as much as possible with everything from feeding to bathing him; I did everything except administer his medication. He had to regain his motor skills. It was a tough thing to watch. When you see a loved one go from being strong, vibrant and alive like Mike, to not being able to lift a spoon or walk, it can be hard to witness. It was an emotional test. This would be another faith fight. Despite the odds being stacked against him, with the insinuation that he would never return to normal, we still believed God for complete and total healing. We did not let up on our Operation Faith strategy either. My family and our close friends continued to strategically pray, using God's Word as our guide. I had to stand on the Word more than ever. I had to pray powerful promises found in scripture over Mike's healing. I had to continue doing what we had done to get us to this point.

Despite being in treatment for several days, he still wasn't moving very well or walking just yet. I remember one day Dr. Smith and her sister Toni were in Mike's room while I went to get food and he received a visit from a physician, who had not been as close to his faith recovery process or our family as the other staff. This physician was extremely negative, and as she was speaking with Mike, she said, "If you ever walk again, you will…" Well, Mike cut her off, because that "if" got him FIRED UP. He threw his hands up and yelled, **"Do you think that I want to be like this?"** Everyone was shocked, because he had not moved his hands up until that point. In that moment, if I or anyone else had any doubts that Mike would make a full recovery he would have silenced them right then. Everyone was in still shock (in a good way) when I returned. "He told her," Dr. Smith thought. More importantly, he had moved his arms for the first time! That doctor soon changed that negative language, and the staff at the rehab facility became a part of our faith-filled army. This proved that faith, determination, and anger with the enemy can work wonders for our will power. I also realized how strong Mike's spirit man was, despite his physical state. As I mentioned earlier "if" is often a word of doubt, and the enemy is slick. He will often plant that doubt in us by way of others. Mike's spirit picked up on that trickster and shut it down. The words that we speak over our lives are extremely important; so do not allow people to speak things over you that are not consistent with what you are believing God for. Pocket that because that is a faith principle!

Have you ever been so close to seeing a promise, yet it still seemed so far away? This is how the transitional process that we were in felt at times. We knew he would be coming home, but we still had a ways to go before we reached that promised land.

CREATE MEMORIES

Despite how trying this process was, while we were in rehab, our attitudes remained positive. One day, Brittney reminded me, "Mom this process doesn't have to be stressful. Let's create some memories while we're here." I reminded Mike of this every chance I got. I assured him that the promise was in sight, but we just had to stay in the process, and make the best of things. One time I told him we were going out on a date. We actually had regular "date nights" in that rehab room. I would put him in the lift, moving him from the bed to the chair so that he could sit up. I transformed the room – washing the walls, and cleaning up, doing my best to make it as comfortable as possible. I brought in a television with a Roku stick, so that he could watch whatever he wanted.

I purchased a DVD player and a television so we could have movie night. I brought one of those Bluetooth speakers so we could listen to music. I made it comfortable enough, so that whatever we needed was right there, but not so comfortable that we wanted to stay.

I knew that crab legs were Mike's favorite, so I went out to Red Lobster and brought some back to his room. Then we took pictures together and I fed the crab legs to him. During another one of our dates, I made a vision board for his wall. I asked him the things that he wanted to do once he got out of rehab, and then I found pictures that conveyed his visions and pinned them to the board. I made sure that each and every desire was represented on that board. I even put a purse up there for me, and told him when he got out I wanted him to buy it for me (I got that purse too!). I wanted to keep things going, and be intentional about creating memories for our testimony. The last thing I wanted to do was return to regular life and the church and tell everyone that I wasted three and a half months being down in the dumps, crying and sobbing about how bad Mike's situation looked. I documented things because I knew we were both coming out of this alive. This was a bold move. People who do not believe that the outcome will be in their favor, will not have the guts to take pictures during times of great trials. They can't be focused on the end. They are only focused on the present and how they feel in that moment. Which leads to another faith principle for you:

Do not ever let what you see today, prevent you from getting to your tomorrow. Many are superstitious about sharing their faith. They think, the less I say, the less I will be embarrassed about if what I am hoping for does not come to pass. Well I am telling you to say it, shout it, take pictures of it, video record it. Do whatever you have to do to convince yourself that your faith will make you whole.

We had our trying moments during this time too. One night I was so outdone with him. He thought I was being too rough when I was moving his covers. He started fussing at me, and I started fussing back at him; until finally he said, "Go home! Go home!" He cried. I cried, and through my frustrated tears I yelled back, "I'm not going home!" It was tough. I got on his nerves and he got on mine. That was a challenging time during our transition, but it only lasted that moment. What I realize is that it was not about me at all, he was simply tired of dealing with this. He wanted out so I had to calm down and FOCUS.

I became committed to keeping our spirits up. It is important to keep your joy in tact when you are in a process, and especially after God gives you a glimpse of the promise, as He had done with us. If you have joy, you will have strength, but if the devil can steal your joy, he can also steal your strength. You need *spiritual* strength to make it to the finish line. This spiritual strength Mike had practiced through a life of faith enabled him to recover faster than normal. While he was weak physically, he was stronger than ever spiritually. As I have mentioned, we cannot fight the physical battles that the enemy puts us through in the natural world—we must fight them in the spiritual. If you apply the faith principles mentioned in this book, you can develop the spiritual stamina to keep going. During this process, I kept my joy, and never stopped being me, a minister, teacher and faith-filled believer in Christ. Even in the rehab center, our faith brought people to Jesus. We stayed on task and focused on faith, even during the process.

TRANSFORMATION

After Jesus' resurrection, when he showed Himself to the disciples, and specifically Simon Peter, Jesus asked Peter three times (John 21:17), "Do you love me?" And Peter said yes repeatedly. This was after Peter made the mistake of denying Christ, prior to His death. Jesus told Peter, "If you love Me, feed My sheep." The apostles were in a transitional period at this time—a transition from the painful process of witnessing their Teacher and Savior's crucifixion to now seeing Him post resurrection. Jesus was calling Peter and the others to go deeper in their faith—to demonstrate what they had learned, to keep giving. He was calling them to continue their work, by any means necessary. This is what Jesus will do to us during a transition and en route to our promise. He will tell us to "Feed [His] sheep." Peter answered that call, preached during the Pentecost, and became a true leader of the faith.

Will you retreat when the process gets uncomfortable or will you give your all? This will require you to stay in faith, stay positive, and remain dedicated to showing the Jesus in you, even when it gets hard. Once you are saved and in the Word, everything you need to get through a process and transition to your promise is already in you, through the Holy Spirit. For Peter, he simply had to tap into the power of Jesus that was within him. For me, I had to stay connected to the Jesus in me and never lose my joy and my will to "feed the sheep." If you love Jesus, you will feed His sheep as well. Instead of worrying about the process or transition period that you are in, search within and discover what Jesus is calling you to do. Go deeper. You have the authority to do so. Jesus transitioned the disciples (followers) to "apostles" (teachers). He elevated them. While Mike was in rehab, I experienced a transition as well. My behavior and strength were an example of the authority I gained through Christ and the faith principles that I lived by for so many years. I was able to become an example to others going through a process and demonstrate how to handle the process by staying focused on the promise.

The transitional process you are in now, or the processes you will experience in the future, will indeed prepare you to teach, lead and inspire others to stay faithful toward their promises. Do not give up when you are almost at the finish line. Transition with joy. Feed the sheep. Someone is depending on you to win your fight.

Take your attention off of yourself and put it on someone else's challenge. Before you know it, you will look up and your challenge will be over. When the Scripture tells us to magnify God, it is not because God has an ego problem. He understands when we magnify Him it decreases our situation. It changes our perspective. So make Him bigger than your problem in your own eyes, and watch your problem disappear.

FAITH PRINCIPLE EIGHT

Sometimes it will get harder before it gets easier. Never lose your joy when you are in transition. Instead, search within to discover how you can continue giving to others and preparing your testimony for God's glory.

Even during a difficult process, look for ways to "say yes" and help others, to demonstrate the love of Jesus through your actions. How can you feed His sheep? How can you walk in the authority that you have through Christ Jesus?

WORD WEAPON

"For we are His workmanship, created in Christ Jesus for good works, which God prepared beforehand that we should walk in them."

Ephesians 2:10

NINE
THE PROMISE PERSPECTIVE

Many people go through life believing God for one promise only - the promise of salvation: *if you confess with your mouth the Lord Jesus and believe in your heart that God has raised Him from the dead, you will be saved* (Romans 10:9). This promise is undoubtedly the most important promise that anyone can ever receive. And similarly the coinciding promise of grace—*For by grace you have been saved through faith, and that not of yourselves; it is the gift of God, not of works, lest anyone should boast.* (Ephesians 2:8-9).

If you do not know any other promises from God, the promises of salvation and God's grace are your *blessed assurance* that your life here is not all you have to look forward to. However, without realizing the thousands of other promises from God—that He made to you, you will have a limited view of God and yourself, and not only that, but you will underestimate God. As a result, you will underestimate the power you have through Him. Until you view life and your processes from a promise perspective, you will not live life to its full potential. I was able to view the process of my husband being ill from a promise perspective, because Gods' Word abided in me, and I saw the circumstance from the perspective of Gods' Word. This is a powerful position to fight from, and it is a position that you too can adopt - meditation.

There are two types of promises that God makes to us, through His Word. A conditional promise - meaning something has to happen, prior to us receiving that promise. To receive God's conditional promises, we have to do something, more specifically, we have to obey Christ's instructions. Notice the condition in the promise of salvation from Romans 10:9. *If you confess... and believe...* The word "if" lets you know that you have to do something in order to receive this promise from God. On the other hand, an unconditional promise means that God is making a guarantee, regardless of our actions. Throughout the 66 books of the Bible, there are over 3,000 promises written, both conditional and unconditional. An example of an unconditional promise in the Bible is the covenant between God and creation in Gen. 8:21, *"... Then the LORD said in His heart, "I will never again curse the ground for man's sake, although the imagination of man's heart is evil from his youth; nor will I again destroy every living thing as I have done."* The Lord also made an unconditional promise to Abraham in Genesis 15:5, *"Look now toward the heaven, and count the stars if you are able to number them." And He said to him, "So shall your descendants be."* After this, as a result of Abraham's obedience, and his willingness to sacrifice his only son Isaac as instructed by God, the Lord made him another unconditional promise in Genesis 22:18, *"In your seed all the nations of the earth shall be blessed, because you have obeyed My voice."*

Many of the conditional promises that God makes in the Bible are based on the condition of obedience—or faith. In Matthew 11:28, Jesus promises to give us rest *if* we come to Him, *"Come to me, all who labor and are heavy laden, and I will give you rest."* We also have the conditional promise of forgiveness, *"For if you forgive others their trespasses, your heavenly Father will also forgive you, but if you do not forgive others their trespasses, neither will your Father forgive your trespasses"* (Matt. 6:14-15). We are also promised endless possibilities if we believe (Mark 9:23). And in Deuteronomy 11:26-28, God promises to bless (or curse us) depending on if we obey Him or not, *"See, I am setting before you today a blessing and a curse: the blessing, if you obey the commandments of the Lord your God, which I command you today, and the curse, if you do not obey the commandments of the Lord your God, but turn aside from the way that I am ..."*

The conditional and unconditional promises of God, written by the prophets of the Bible under the direction of God are still relevant today, and it is up to us to seek and reap them. Just as God spoke to the writers of the Bible, He speaks to us today. If you believe God has given you a promise, through a vision, a dream, a quiet whisper, or confirmation, search the Scriptures to see what God has said and wants to say to you regarding what you are believing Him for. As you grow in the Word, it will become easier to recognize the voice of God. You won't doubt when Holy Spirit is speaking to you after a while. You'll "just know."

This was true for me. Throughout our process, I just knew that certain promises were directly from God, whether they were given to me through Holy Spirit or by way of my niece, Dr. Nikia Wooten, my daughters Brittney or Brelyn, or whether I found a Word in the Bible that I prayed over Mike's health. The Lord's voice becomes clear to His followers (John 10:27), and His promises are true. I knew that God promised healing for Mike. This was confirmed through Gods' Word, and I resided and abided in these promises to sustain me during the process.

PROMISES OF HEALING

Behold, I will bring it health and healing; I will heal them and reveal to them the abundance of peace and truth.

Jeremiah 33:6

The Lord will strengthen him on his bed of illness; You will sustain him on his sickbed.

Psalm 41:3

Is anyone among you sick? Let him call for the elders of the church, and let them pray over him, anointing him with oil in the name of the Lord.

James 5:14

But He was wounded for our transgressions, He was bruised for our iniquities; The chastisement for our peace was upon Him, And by His stripes we are healed.

Isaiah 53:5

God made a conditional promise to us in Romans 8:28. It is one of my favorite promises, because the only condition is that we love Him, *"And we know that all things work together for good to those who love God, to those who are the called according to His purpose."* The important point about promises that I want you to remember is that God cannot lie. Once you know and believe the magnitude of this truth, you will never doubt God's promises for your life and situation again.

WHEN THE PROMISE IS NEAR

When the promise is near, the process tends to get very difficult, frustrating and discouraging. I know you may have heard or experienced this before: right before your breakthrough, you often want to breakdown. Take Abraham, whom God told to sacrifice his chosen son Isaac. Abraham went so far as to strap Isaac to the rock, and was ready to obey God and sacrifice his son, when God stopped him right in the knick of time. In Genesis 22:18 we see that this test had consequences that affected the course of the whole world, including the lives that you and I live today, "In your seed all the nations of the earth shall be blessed, because you have obeyed My voice." Abraham obeyed God, and He blessed him abundantly with one of the greatest promises of all time.

It is important that you get this. When you feel like breaking down during the process, you have two choices: give up and forego the God ordained outcome, or continue to fight and experience the promise that you have been praying for. Your choice will determine which way things go for you. If you give up, you will set yourself back. Stay in the Word and keep the promise in view.

When Mike was in rehab, there was a point when this whole situation really started to get to him. He was so ready to come home. One evening, my brother-in-law Dwayne, sister-in-law Lisa, and my parents came to his room and sat with him for a long time. It was getting late, and they were like, "Okay we're getting ready to go…" In that moment, tears welled up in his eyes and he began to cry. It was an emotional moment for us all. He was so frustrated, and it was not that he doubted that he would return home. He was just tired and fed up with this process. He had had enough. I knew I had to change his mind and what he was thinking. I had to remind him that this was a temporary situation. Although we listened to worship music and sing everyday, take pictures, and enjoy visitors, the time confined in the hospital and now rehab had taken a toll on him. In that moment, he just needed my encouragement. I need the wisdom of Holy Spirit and in order to tap into it I had to go deeper in my worship.

I always knew that I was a worshipper, but this situation took me to another level of worship. Worshipping God was how I was able to keep my mind off of what was going on with Mike. It was also where I received more spiritual strength to continue to be an encourager despite how frustrating things were. I knew what was going on with him, but my spirit man was totally engulfed in the presence of God, because that was where my strength would come from. One of the songs that stuck with me during this time was Canton Jones' "Worshipper." In that song, he talks about worshipping God in an elevator and on a respirator, and I thought "who would write that (respirator) in a song?" I knew it had to be God who sent that song to me, because I had never heard it before. I would sing it everyday, "They don't know that I'm a worshipper. They don't know that I'm in love with you..." Seriously, worship kept me strong.

If you experience a moment in your process where you want to breakdown, do not try to go through it alone. If you do not have an encourager there to help lift your spirits, stand on the promises of God, and go deeper in your worship. Let the Lord minister to you.

STAND ON A PROMISE

I have come to learn that God's conditional promises can be

quite rewarding. Conditional promises require us to work—to activate faith, trust and take some risks (or what we consider to be risks). In the natural, it is often said, "the bigger the natural risk, the bigger the reward," right? Well just imagine the spiritual rewards associated with the risks you take in faith.

While Mike was in rehab, after he had gone through weeks of intense physical therapy, he began to show promising signs. He was starting to walk again, and his speech had returned. He was now eating on his own, and breathing much better than before. He began to get antsy and wanted to know exactly when he could go home. I remember asking the doctors, who did not want to let him go at first. A nurse came in at one point, after we had not yet received any definitive answer from the other physicians and we asked her if she could ask the doctor to release him. She said that Mike could probably be released, on two conditions: that he take his oxygen machine home with him, and continue rehab. Well, we put our faith on those conditional promises. A few days later, Mike went into therapy, and the doctor came in and told me that he could be released. While he was in therapy, I packed up his things, so that I could surprise him when he returned to the room. When he completed his physical therapy that day, Mike made his way back down to the room, and all of the nurses were in the hallway cheering him on and giving him high five's. Some of them were crying, because they were happy to see him go. You could visibly see the manifestation of weeks and months of this promise build up on Mike's face as he slowly smiled. He realized why we were celebrating. We held each other and cried tears of joy. It was finally time to live in God's promise—completely! He was going home. This moment made me emotional as well. Once I saw that huge grin on Mike's face, I too finally released all of the emotions that had been bottled up, and cried. Those were the best tears of joy I have ever shed.

Some will read this story and think that these promises only apply to our lives. Or maybe you are thinking that the Freemans' are somehow "lucky" or favored. While we are favored and blessed, you need to realize that you are too. Do not let the enemy play those games with your mind. Remember the promise of God's Word, which states, "For God does not show favoritism" (Romans 2:11 NLT). These lessons about faith and God's promises are for everyone to grab ahold of. You can never go wrong by having a promise perspective. When you are focused on God's promises, versus your problems, you are closer to a solution, because you are directly hooked up with the problem solver Himself. For the average person, giving up is easier than remaining faithful. They quit in the process, not realizing that they have a Father that promised to never leave them nor forsake them, and would move heaven and earth to see them through their trial. Giving up during a process is just like giving up on God, and telling Him that He is a liar and you do not believe the contract He made with you (the Bible) full of His promises. If you give up on God during this process, how will God be able to trust you for what He has planned for you in the next season? My prayer is that you endure hardship as a good soldier. In the name of Jesus, I pray that you will no longer think or behave as an average person, who gives up during a process. Instead, realize that you are a daughter or son of God, and therefore, there is always an answer waiting for you if you will stop and just listen. God has created you to win.

FAITH PRINCIPLE NINE

Right before you are going to walk in your promise, your process will get extremely difficult. You cannot give up. Look for a promise to stand on, and be ready to do your part!

Is there a lesson God's been trying to teach you about obedience or faith, in order for you to see the promises He has for your life? What do you have to give up in order to be obedient to God and walk in your promise and purpose? It might be over spending, over promising to others without following through, fornication, telling lies. Think about it, and write it down, before you continue to the next chapter.

WORD WEAPON

"If you are willing and obedient, You shall eat the good of the land."

Isaiah 1:19

TEN
A PROCESS PREPARES, A PROMISE SUSTAINS

In 2012, prior to going on stage to teach during the God's Glamorous Girls Conference that I host, I asked God to reveal who I would be speaking to that day. He placed it in my spirit that someone in that room was fighting the demon of suicide. I know how to speak to suicide, because I too have experienced those feelings of wanting to die—even asking God to take me out.

I used to wish I could die. I used to think of ways to kill myself. I used to cry so much, and wish terrible things on myself, like, "God, maybe I can have an aneurysm in my brain…." The devil will paint pictures for you about how you are about to die, especially if you are helping him out by asking for it! He will also show you how you can just take yourself out. I used to think about pills as well. Then I realized I did not know which pills to take, and just my luck, I'd end up sick the next day, but still alive. Then I would think about using a gun, but I was too afraid. I did not want to experience the agony associated with shooting myself in the face. Again, what if I did it wrong? Then I considered driving myself into a collision. I put myself through all this mental agony because I did not like the situation that I was in. I did not like the process that I was in, and I wanted to bail out, and quick! So many women and men that I encounter can relate to these feelings, and if you are one of them, I want you to know that you do not have to be ashamed. You are still here, and that means that God is not done with you yet. Remember what I told you in the last chapter? God created you to win. So let's go deeper into God's promises for your life.

    When I learned that I could fight and win I started refusing to lose. Meditation is one of the most empowering things you can do. The world teaches you to detach from everything, to release and live in the moment. However, the Bible teaches us to attach to His Word when we meditate. When you look up any scripture about meditation it's always attached to the precepts and laws. Philippians 4:8 NKJV says, "... *whatever things are true, whatever things are noble, whatever things are just, whatever things are pure, whatever things are lovely, whatever things are of good report, if there is any virtue and if there is anything praiseworthy—meditate on these things."*. We have to attach our thoughts to God's Word so we can become one with it. Meditation is not something to just cause us to rest and relax but God gave it to us to win in every area of our lives.

When I wanted to check out of life I had to train myself through the Word to think differently. I started to meditate on scriptures like I Peter 5:7, *"casting all your care upon Him, for He cares for you"* and II Corinthians 2:14, *"Now thanks be to God who always leads us in triumph in Christ..."* I began to live in these scriptures, seeing myself giving all of the bad thoughts and challenges I was going through to the Father, knowing that He has caused me to be triumphant in all things. It is impossible to lose when you stand on God's Word.

This is my life; so living by the Word is not optional for me. Going to church and attending Bible study is another non-negotiable for me. Many Christians are deciding to live life outside of the biblical guidelines set forth in the Word of God, and it is pretty sad to see. Only because I know as soon as tragedy hits they will come running to the same place they ran away from. When I was going through hard times I never disconnected from fellowship. This is how I have always been able to transition from pain to pleasure; from seeing death to starting to live in the abundant life God promised me. Let me encourage you to stick to what you know is right so the enemy will not be able to toss you to and fro. It is time to be planted in this great gospel. Get established in a great church that will teach you faith and how to believe God.

Specifically, I want you to realize that your processes can prepare you for what is next, and your promise-focused mindset will sustain you through whatever you are going through. This is a strategy that never fails, no matter what you are facing.

I want you to circle 2 Corinthians 1:20 in your Bible, which states, *"For all the promises of God in him are yes, and in him Amen, to the glory God through us."* I love this verse because God was sure to emphasize "all." All promises of God are yes and amen. It doesn't say some or just a few, or the ones that we remember. It says "all." I believe that if you get a revelation of just this one scripture (even if you have not followed along with me and read the entire book) that by the Spirit of God, 2 Corinthians 1:20 would be enough to sustain you. Think about it this way. If you know that all your needs are met, and God promised to meet them, what else is there? I may not know you personally, but I am almost sure that most of your struggles and your stress come from not knowing if God is going to do exactly what He said He would do.

You are stressed because you do not know if your needs will be met. Let me help you out a little bit: 1 Kings 8:56 says, *"Blessed be the Lord, who has given rest to His people Israel, according to all that He promised. There has not failed one word of all His good promise, which He promised through His servant Moses."*

Okay, so I want you to follow me… All of God's promises are yes. And then He backed it up, and reassured us that there has not been one failed promise. So, if this is true, (and I use "if" rhetorically since we know that God cannot lie), I want you to ask yourself a question: *Why is it that I don't see what I want to see in my life God, when You said You promised me certain things? So is it You, God, or is it me?* I want to remind you of Genesis 8:22, *"While the earth remains, Seedtime and harvest, cold and heat, winter and summer, and day and night shall not cease."* Understand that there must be time in between seed and harvest. I sow my seed, then there is time, and then I receive my harvest. God did not say how long it was going to take for your harvest (or mine) to manifest. I am telling you that it is going to take time to see the harvest. That time right there really should be referred to as "process." Because in order to see a harvest, your seed must go through a process.

I am not sure if you were like me and ever planted something when you were in school. You remember you got a milk carton from your teacher? You cut the top part off. You got a little bit of dirt and then the teacher gave you some seeds to plant. You set those planted seeds by the window, and the next day you went to school to check on your seed to see if anything had sprouted. You followed this same routine day after day, and nothing. It did not begin to sprout immediately. Everyday you would go back to school and you would watch that thing grow. You would begin to see a little bit sprout up through the dirt, and you got excited. You did not understand, or really see, what that seed was doing inside of the dirt, did you? It was going through a process. Most Christians do not like processes. The Word itself sounds like something that will take a lot of time. We know we are an impatient, impetuous people. We do things so quickly. We want it quick, fast and in a hurry. When it comes to the plan of God, or to the order of God, we want to see things take place just that fast.

    Let me give you an example of how a promise sustains me each year during what sometimes looks like a chaotic time. I like Christmas. It's my favorite time of the year. Pastor Mike tells everybody how, "Christmas could be all year long for DeeDee." Every year I have about a hundred or so of my family members come over my house. We sit around the Christmas tree, and we eat all kinds of food, drink virgin eggnog, and we have so much fun. People even have come to identify me by my love for Christmas trees.

If I could put my tree up in September, I would. But that would be ridiculous, so I make sure to get it up in October before Thanksgiving. My awesome sister Darnice is the absolute best decorator and knows how much I love Christmas trees. She also knows it's a lot of work that has to be put in to put my tree up. The tree is about 20 feet tall, and it takes about two to three days just to put the branches on. They bring in scaffolds and ladders to put this thing together. If you come in my foyer during this time, you will see stuff all over the place. There are big boxes everywhere because the ornaments themselves are like the size of a human head. During this time, I cannot bring any outsiders in the house because there is just that many items. As annoying as it may be to me sometimes, I never, ever, ever ,(let me repeat) ever, say to her that I don't want the tree anymore. I never stop the process because I do not like all this stuff laid out in the foyer; because it takes too long to put up; because I cannot invite anybody over; not even because other people are going to say and think negative about me when they see all this junk in my house. I have never told my sister to stop decorating and the workers to stop putting the tree together. Do you want to know why? Because I love Christmas. I love Christmas trees. And the promise of the finished product sustains me. Thinking about the end result gives me patience, peace, joy, and happiness.

THE PROCESS PREPARES. THE PROMISE SUSTAINS.

I like my tree. I like what I see. I love all of the decorations. I love the beauty of it. I love getting to the end of the process, where everybody else can come and say, "Wow!" You might not like Christmas. That may not be your thing, but if you're a woman you can probably relate to an example that has to do with something we all have - hair. As a licensed cosmetologist I did hair for eighteen years. And every time a client would come in, I always had to check to see if she had any new growth (virgin hair growing from the scalp). I would check to determine whether or not she needed a relaxer, or "touch-up."

I would check the scalp, and in most cases, I would notice that she needed a touch-up. A lot of times my clients would tell me they did not need a touch up saying, "No, it's only been about three weeks." And I would look at the records and say, "No, it's been six to seven weeks. You need a touch-up." And after going back and forth for a few minutes, they would agree. I would begin by basing their scalp and putting the petroleum jelly between each layer of hair along the scalp. Then I would apply the relaxer to their hair. If they scratched or had abrasions before

I started after a while I would see tears rolling down their faces because the chemicals would begin to burn. Their legs would start to shake hard and they would be begging me to hurry up. I would say, "Hey, you want me to take it out? I can wash it out right now. We can stop. I don't want you to have scabs on your scalp." I would even offer to spray some oil sheen or water in the hair. Yet not one time, in eighteen years, did I have a client jump out of the chair and say they no longer wanted to go through the process of getting the relaxer. You know why? Because they saw themselves at the end of the process, leaving out of that salon, with their hair blowing in the wind. Or if they had short hair it being laid down in the back. They did not want to pay all of that money, get out of that chair, and not finish the process.

Why is it that when we are believing God for something great in our lives and in the lives of our loved ones, we are so quick to get in the process and bail out when it begins to hurt and burn? If you are not willing to endure a little discomfort or extreme pain, you are not ready for the promise.

I read this story about this ancient Indian sage who taught the art of archery. He had two guys with him, and he was going to teach them how to shoot with the bow and arrow. He told the first one to get up. "I'm going to place this wooden bird back there on that tree stump. And

I want you to aim for one of the eyes of the bird. And when you see it, that is what I want you to hit." So, he called the guy up, and he said okay what do you see? The first one said, "I see the eyes of the bird. I see it's feathers. I see the tree stump. I even see some leaves and stuff blowing over there cause it's a little windy." He saw everything around the target. So the Indian sage told him to step to the side, and he brought the other guy up. "What do you see?" he asked the second guy. He responded, "I see the eye of the bird." The instructor was a little surprised, so he asked him again. The guy reiterated, "I see the eye of the bird." So the Indian sage told him, "Okay, you are ready to shoot." So, the first guy looked and said, "I saw his eyes as well," but the teacher corrected him, and said, "Until you are able to only focus on what you are aiming for, you will never hit your target." This is what I want to remind you of. Until you are able to focus on what you are aiming for, you will never, EVER hit your target.

    Most Christians are all over the place. One minute we are up, the next minute we are down. One minute we are going to believe God, and the next minute we are not. What is your breaking point? What will cause you to lose your focus? Are you going to believe God or not? The devil has turned up the heat. This is not the time for Christians to bow down and be unaware of who they are in Christ Jesus. This is not the time to pull back from your church, your business, or your relationship. If you are going to do anything, you need to press in and lean in to the Word of God like never before. Just like the devil has turned up the heat, God has turned up the heat as well. He is pouring out His Spirit on you like never before. But only if you believe. It is time for you to see miracles. I am not sure about you, but I do not want to just talk about miracles, or hear a preacher prophesy about miracles. I want to see miracles, and not so I can believe, but because I *do* believe. Don't you want to see them?

When Pastor Mike was going through this process, I already told you how I told God, "If you are God, and if You really keep Your Word, I want to see the manifestation of it in my life. I am not going to waver. I am not going to bow down. I am not going to cower back, but I am going to lean in, until I see it manifest in my life." Some of us get to the place where it is just *oh so hard*. You hurt so bad. You just want to leave. You do not want this anymore. Yes, this may be true for you, but it is not time to quit if you want better.

It is not time to quit. Repeat after me: It is not time to quit. It is not time to quit. It is not time to quit! Let that sink into your spirit.

PAIN TO RECOVERY

Most people do not like the pain of recovery. It is truly painful to recover. Think about anyone who has broken a leg and they have to go through therapy. Anybody who has had any type of surgery knows that it is a painful process. People do not like pain, and so they do not endure. Everybody likes pleasure, but sometimes pain comes before pleasure. We all understand that God does not require us to go through painful situations to enjoy pleasure, but in life there are painful situations that will occur and you have to be willing to endure that hardship like a good soldier in order to get to the end results. For Mike, it was painful to breathe and to workout at the same time. It would hurt in his chest, and that pain was real, but he never quit. He went to therapy seven days a week. They would have to put him in this lift. He was not even walking, but they would move his legs so that he could get a visual and could begin to associate the muscle-brain functions of how it felt to move his legs. There were times when he had to ride a bike and they would strap his arms and legs to the bike when he could not peddle for himself. He knew that if he wanted to ever walk again, and be back to his normal self, he would have to endure that pain.

One thing I have noticed about most people is that they focus on what they are going through and not what they are going to. Let me explain something to you - you will not find any scripture in the Bible that promises us that the process will be smooth or that the process will be without challenges. Nowhere does God say the process will be easy. Look at the story of Noah. God told him that it was going to rain, but if he would obey Him and build an ark for the saving of his family, they would be spared from the tribulation that was coming on the earth. I am quite sure it was not comfortable or easy being on a boat with hundreds of animals for forty days, and I am certain it did not smell too nice. God did not zap them off the earth and completely spare them from the impending trouble, but He promised that Hhe would see them through it if they trusted Him. Do you trust Him enough to endure your storm?

You have to allow the process to prepare you, while keeping your eyes on the promise. It will sustain you. You will see that God has guaranteed His promises. So, why focus on something that He has never guaranteed you? Hoping and wishing things will be easy is simply a waste of your time. Focus on what He has promised you. I know it's hard. I know it is a lot of work, but it is a good fight. Why? Because we win. We win the fight. All you have to do is show up. All you have to do is show up for your fight. It is already won. God has fixed the fight to end up in your favor, if you simply show up and fight. Most of us do not like the pressure. We do not like the heat, and we do not like the troubles. We like it just the way it is, comfy. So we avoid the fight altogether. This is why Christians die early or go through all of the junk that they go through; they are not willing to stand in the process. Romans 4:19 in the Message Bible, says that *Abraham didn't focus on his own impotence and say, "It's hopeless. This hundred-year-old body could never father a child." Nor did he survey Sarah's decades of infertility and give up. He didn't tiptoe around God's promise, asking cautiously, skeptical questions. He plunged into the promise and came up strong, ready for God, sure that God would make good on what he had said.*

You have read this book about God's promises up until this point because this message is for you. Yes it may really hurt and I totally understand your pain but when you are about to fall out of the process, when you are about to throw in the towel, you have to know that God has given you a Word to sustain you. *Abraham plunged into the promise and he came up strong, ready for God.* But, verse 21 (in Genesis 17) is the key. Abraham was sure that God would make good on what He said. Abraham did not look at his own ability to carry out what God said. Remember that you must trust God. You must know what to focus on. Do not focus on the process. Focus on the promise.

We have a member at our church that is in law enforcement and is an excellent shooter. Well, one day she came to my house to show me how to shoot. She began to teach me about this gun. She said, "These are the things you need to identify and know about before you shoot this gun. This is the rear sight. This is the front sight, and then there is your visual. Like your target." And I repeated, "There is a rear sight, a front sight and then your visual, which is your target, is that right?" This is what she said next, "All you need to do is line up your rear sight with your front sight, to what you want to shoot." I shook my head in agreement. She was speaking my language. In that moment, God began to speak to me. I heard God say, *Okay your rear sight is what you are closest to—your circumstances, your situations, the stuff that you can see the best. He said the front sight is the word of God. This is what you line it up with.* He said and *your target is whatever you're going after to see change.* I said okay. She begins goes on to say, "You know you are never able to focus on both sights and your target at the same time." I asked her what she meant by that. She said, "Once you line up your rear sight and your front sight, you take your sight off of the rear sight and you place it on your front sight. You aim it towards your target, but you never have to put your sight on the target again." She continued, "Your primary focus comes off of your target and it goes on your front sight." That was confirmation!

  I know you cannot hear me through these pages, but I need you to read and understand it as if I am speaking to YOU! It is impossible for you to focus on your circumstances and your situations while simultaneously focusing on the Word of God. One of them is going to trump the other. You have to be willing to focus on what God told you to focus on and not on what you see. Listen, the front sight on the gun is so small in comparison to what you will ever be shooting at. My point is this: your circumstances and challenges may appear to be overwhelming in comparison to the amount of Word you know, but take your eyes off of what you are going through and put it on the Word. Be like Abraham and focus on the promise. Declare right here for yourself: I'm going to focus on the promises of God.

FAITH PRINCIPLE TEN

If you keep your focus on the promise, it will sustain you during a process. Until you can focus on what you are aiming for, you will never hit your target.

What are your specific goals right now? Check your focus, every minute of everyday. People are often distracted by the world—social media, what others are doing, lies the devil tell (such as you are not doing enough or you are a failure because it looks like you are not doing as well as others). If you take your focus off of these distractions and put them back on your promise, you will hit your target—guaranteed.

WORD WEAPON

"Enter by the narrow gate; for wide is the gate and broad is the way that leads to destruction, and there are many who go in by it. 14 Because [a] narrow is the gate and difficult is the way which leads to life, and there are few who find it."

Matthew 7:13-14

ELEVEN
WELCOME HOME

As we drove up the driveway, we could hear the screams and cheers from down the road. Our brothers, sisters, nieces, nephews, children, extended family, in-laws, friends and closest church family were there to welcome Mike home, cheering with excitement. The support from our family was just beautiful. Once we got Mike out of the car, we cried together. It was an emotional moment. Everyone gathered around, giving hugs, gifts, and balloons. We snapped photos and simply enjoyed one another. I know that God was smiling on us. We had fought a faith fight and won. Mike had been gone for three and a half months by this time. And finally, he was home.

It feels so good to see your faith manifest in real life and see the promise right there live and in the flesh. For it to happen in such a way that it could not be denied or discounted, made it all the better.

God would get all the glory. We had a testimony, Mike and I, and so did our Spirit of Faith family. For years we had taught our church partners how to live by faith and walk in the spirit. We were surely tested. One major lesson to take away from this time is that processes shape us. They refine us, strengthen us and when we come out of a process, things are never the same as they were before the process began. God is not a trouble-maker. He does not bring you trouble to make you stronger or to teach you a lesson. But there is a lesson in your trouble.

    Prior to Mike being released from the hospital, the doctors told him that he would need to continue his rehab treatment at home. I am certain he heard and understood their instructions. And while I know he would have agreed to just about anything to be released from that hospital, when we got home, it was a different story. Mike wanted to abort the process and abandon the two conditions that led to his release from the hospital - rehab and his use of the oxygen as well. Before I share the details of this ordeal, let me pause for a quick teaching moment. Oftentimes when we are in a process, God will show us a glimpse of the promise. This was true for the Israelites, who wandered the wilderness for 40 years after God released them from the treacherous reality of slavery at the hand of the Egyptian Pharaoh. When they were close to their promised land, God spoke to Moses and told him to send spies to scout out the land of Canaan that He had promised them. They were able to get a glimpse of the promise, and shape their behavior accordingly. All of the spies, except for two, returned with bad reports, and began to murmur against Aaron and Moses, wishing they were back in Egypt. They lacked faith and because the people who occupied the land of Canaan appeared to be stronger, they were ready to abort the process God was taking them through. But two of the men who scouted the land, Joshua and Caleb, had faith in God despite what things looked like in the natural.

Numbers 14:6-9 reads:

"But Joshua the son of Nun and Caleb the son of Jephunneh, who were among those who had spied out the land, tore their clothes; and they spoke to all the congregation of the children of Israel, saying: "The land we passed through to spy out is an exceedingly good land. If the Lord delights in us, then He will bring us into this land and give it to us, 'a land which flows with milk and honey.' Only do not rebel against the Lord, nor fear the people of the land, for they are our bread; their protection has departed from them, and the Lord is with us. Do not fear them."

Joshua and Caleb understood that they were in a position of strength. By getting a glimpse of the promised land, they were able to prepare for things to come. Oftentimes God will give us a glimpse of the promise to encourage us to continue on. But, if we lose faith like the Israelites, we delay the promise even more. In Galatians 6:9 the Bible cautions us against growing weary in well doing, reminding us that *"in due season, we will reap if we faint not."* When you get a glimpse of the promise, do not draw back in fatigue, instead, perservere until you receive the manifestation. We are to take our cue from Joshua and Caleb and stand in faith.

Mike was able to return home on the condition that he would keep up his rehab. This conditional promise was a glimpse of the full-fledge promise that God had in store. It was not time to abandon the process. His continued participation in rehab was a part of the required process that would lead to the promise. This was our *conditional* promise.

One day, the physical therapists came to our house to begin Mike's treatments, and he was not having it. When I tell you this was an ordeal - honey listen! He moaned, "What are these people coming into my house for? I do not need anymore treatments." In that moment, he truly wanted to believe that he was done with treatment. Can you imagine what this was like for me? We had come too far for him to get out of the process and start backsliding now, so he had some decisions to make. Either he was going to focus on how he was feeling at the present time, or he could focus on the end goal - a life without oxygen tanks, home visits from therapists, or even routine trips to the doctor's office. It is tempting for us to want to abort the process when we experience a small victory. I see people do this all the time when it looks like their marriage is better or they get a new house or get healed. After experiencing such a victory, they stop coming to church. I am not satisfied with half a victory. I want to be like the leper that turned around to say thank you to Jesus for healing him and Jesus made him whole in every area. I want it all! We were not quite at our promise land yet, and I needed my husband to get a grip! The physical therapist came in to meet Mike, but he refused to come out of the room. I got on the phone and called my pastor, Apostle Price, and told him, "Mike is not coming out of the room. You need to talk to him!" I gave Mike the phone. He went back and forth with our pastor for a few minutes, but ultimately he came out to meet the physical therapist. He looked at me and said, "You snitch!" It is funny when I look back at it now. I definitely was a snitch in that moment, because we had come too far to give up on the process! Mike needed to get over himself.

That may be a Word for you as well. Do you need to get over

yourself and stay committed to the process? Do not give up; you are almost there.

PASSION FOR THE PROMISE

Each year during Holy Week, leading up to Good Friday and Resurrection Sunday, Christians pay homage to the great sacrifice Jesus made on our behalf. Churches everywhere watch and reproduce dramas depicting "The Passion" of Jesus Christ. Some of these "Easter" productions are so real they evoke emotions as if you were actually there when Jesus was crucified. I mean, seeing a modern-day Jesus, covered in blood, bearing the cross on this back. One recent production also showed the soldiers, who followed behind Jesus, whipping him on his back as he carried that cross. Have you ever seen a reenactment of the crucifixion that was so real it forced you to imagine the pain that our Savior experienced over 2,000 years ago? And then, to be nailed to a cross, pierced in the side, mocked and chastised as He bled out before a crowd of people who had just been praising and worshipping Him. Talk about betrayal and suffering! John referred to Jesus as "The Lamb of God," who takes away the sin of the world. He was indeed the perfect sacrifice for our redemption. This selfless act was God's way of demonstrating the promise that had been prophesied concerning the

Messiah. Isaiah 53:5 put it this way:

But he was wounded for our transgressions, he was bruised for our iniquities: the chastisement of our peace was upon him; **and with his stripes we are healed.**

"And with his stripes we are healed..." This is the promise that we believed God for concerning Mike's health. His "stripes" refers to the scars Jesus received as He was repeatedly beaten. "By His stripes we are healed," is a promise that we must believe, because it's the very promise that Jesus made to us as He endured the agony of His crucifixion.

When people ask me how I was able to stand so strong, or what I did to stay in my right mind, I tell them exactly what I have told you. It is hard for them to believe that I stood firm on a promise because we judge people from where we are. I want you to understand why I was able to stand so firm. In addition to prayer, worship, and the fact that I kept myself productive, I had to really understand and believe in the promise. Isaiah 53:5 reads, *"But he was wounded for our transgressions, he was bruised for our iniquities: the chastisement of our peace was upon him; and with his stripes we are healed."*

I was on Jesus' mind as His flesh bore that terrible departure from earth. Mike was on His mind when Jesus died for us. "With His stripes we are healed," is not only promising us a Savior from sin, but healing on earth. Jesus died so that Mike could live, and by His stripes, Mike would be healed. I knew this promise was for us.

    Once my husband began to demonstrate authentic signs of healing, it was great because I knew the process was coming to an end. While others were astonished, it was not a surprise to me, because it was what I believed all along. Yes, I was confident in God's promises, but I do not want you to believe it was smooth sailing—even once Mike came home. Things are never the same after a painful process, and we as believers are no exception to this. I am not saying things will be worse, because my life is all the better. Mike does not think the same and he certainly does not view the world the same. I do not either. We are both grateful to have more days to spend together. Everything is beautiful now. Again, you can learn about how to handle your process from the one Jesus went through. Once He died and rose on the third day, things changed for mankind and His disciples. Jesus could no longer walk the earth with them and be as accessible (in the flesh) to the people as He had been in the past. But although He was no longer with them in the flesh, Hhe was with them in the spirit. He died so that He could give a piece of Himself to us all through Holy Spirit, Who now abides in us.

The process Jesus went through changed the entire destiny of mankind. Similarly, our process changed us, as yours has, or will change you. I have realized more than ever that people are in desperate need of faith principles that will enable them to withstand when processes give them more than they are prepared for. The Bible advises us to always be prepared and stay ready to fight the good fight of faith. We are to *live by faith*, not just pick it up when something hits hard. So if you prepare now for a tough process and activate the faith principles we have been discussing, you too will win your fight.

FAITH PRINCIPLE ELEVEN

You will never be the same after a process.

Look forward to a renewed, restored and improved you, with additional insight and more influence!

If you think about some of your dreams, and how big they are, is not it only right that you have to go through some things in order to reach that point in your future? Just like the months of enduring this process, prepared me for a new height in my ministry to travel around the world teaching about the process and the promise, your journey must be preparing you for something BIG.

WORD WEAPON

"And I also say to you that you are Peter, and on this rock I will build My church, and the gates of Hades shall not prevail against it."

Matthew 16:18

TWELVE
FAITHFUL

Earlier I told you how we handled ourselves in the hospital. We were so "different" that we had the doctors and nurses believing God with us—we turned them on to our faith. One day, a nurse saw me praising and worshiping God and said, "How are you able to act like this…. to act how you act?" I replied, "How is that?" She responded, "You are so calm, and you're always smiling, and you're being nice to people…" This was the same lady that I mentioned earlier, who I asked about being saved. So this particular day when she saw me worshipping, she said, "That's how you're able to do this?" And I told her, "Yes, it's all about Jesus." She continued to say, "Well, you know, it's a lot of people around here who don't understand how you are acting. They don't understand how you're able to be happy and calm." So I started singing to this lady. *"They don't know that I'm a worshipper. They don't know that I'm in love with you…"* the Canton Jones' song that I played everyday.

When people see you going through, and you are able to smile, and treat them nicely, and worship despite your circumstances, it will change them too. Worshippers know the outcome. Worshippers know the end results. Worshippers know they win in the end. I do not care how things are appearing, and what is going on in your life, when you can lift up your hands and know that your Heavenly Father, your Daddy, will take care of you, it will bless others. When you know that God is not a man that He should lie, that if He's promised you some things they are going to happen, then you can relax and rest in His presence. That is when you are going to start seeing the results that you want to see. Going through this situation took me to another dimension in my faith. I always knew that nothing was impossible with God, but now it is more than words in THE BOOK. Nothing is impossible with God, *for real*. It is no longer about just quoting scripture or principles that I have been taught. I received *revelation* in my spirit. I saw a man literally brought back to life because of faith. I now know that I am unstoppable through faith. Not because of me. Not because of anything that I have done. Not because I am better than anybody else. I am no better than you. I am not God's special child. I am not His favorite. The only thing I choose to do is believe Him. The difference between me, and those who will not see their results is my choice, and my choice is to believe the Word of the Lord. And I am sharing my testimony to challenge your faith and to encourage you to believe God like you have never done before. Know that God wants to show off in your life if you will just take Him at His Word. It is time to take what the enemy meant for evil, and turn it around and use it for your good–for real this time. Over the next couple of pages, I am going to show you how to make the enemy mad, and please God all the more.

Whether you are single, married, divorced or widowed, from this point forward, I want you to look at yourself as God's significant other. You are in a relationship now. Two important keys to any good relationship are communication and commitment, or *faithfulness*. With God, just like with most relationships, healthy communication will give you the confidence to trust that person enough to be faithful and committed. The more you communicate with God and allow Him to communicate with you, the easier it will become to be faithful. We talked about the importance of prayer earlier, so now let is focus on developing your spirit of faithfulness so that you too can surprise people with your worship the next time you are going through a storm.

Faithfulness means being consistently loyal and trustworthy, with steadfast allegiance. Faithfulness is a fruit of the (Holy) spirit (Gal 5:22-23) that all Christians should display as a result of their walk and growth in Christ. Here are a few verses that describe faithfulness, according to God's Word:

He who is faithful in what is least is faithful also in much; and he who is unjust in what is least is unjust also in much. Therefore if you have not been faithful in the unrighteous mammon, who will commit to your trust the true riches? And if you have not been faithful in what is another man's, who will give you what is your own?
Luke 16:1-12

A faithful man will abound with blessings, But he who hastens to be rich will not go unpunished.
Proverbs 28:20

Moreover it is required in stewards that one be found faithful.

1 Corinthians 4:2

Let not steadfast love and faithfulness forsake you; bind them around your neck; write them on the tablet of your heart. So you will find favor and good success in the sight of God and man.
Proverbs 3:3-4 (ESV)

Because you did not serve the Lord your God with joy and gladness of heart, for the abundance of everything, therefore you shall serve your enemies, whom the Lord will send against you, in hunger, in thirst, in nakedness, and in need of everything; and He will put a yoke of iron on your neck until He has destroyed you."
Deuteronomy 28:47-48

When you are faithful, you will begin to know, love, and trust God. You keep His commandments, and you serve Him despite any obstacle you encounter. When Jesus told Peter, "If you love me, feed my sheep," (John 21:15-17), He was not giving Peter an option. He was reminding Peter how to be faithful in what Jesus had called him to do—to be a shepherd. Let me put this another way for you. You are a teacher, and you wake up one morning feeling down. You decide to go to school anyway and teach your class. Students begin to come in and they are working your last nerve, because you do not feel like being there anyway. Will you let them tend to themselves and continue to misbehave while you sit at your desk, or will you get up and teach your class, discipline your students and take control as the leader of that space? I have heard of and witnessed many pastors losing their place of worship. But they do not quit preaching because they do not have a building. They find another building and continue doing what they are called to do. With the insurgence of the social media app Periscope, I notice a lot of "PeriPreachers," many of whom are not ordained or have church buildings—yet, they feel compelled and passionate about sharing the gospel of Jesus Christ. Some are likely answering a call to be an encourager or evangelist of the gospel. They are not letting their lack of credentials or a building hold them back from being a positive light for others. Again, I am not speaking about all people who preach on Periscope, but some are genuine. When you are faithful, you use what you have to do what God wants you to do. Being faithful is not just about worshipping God and remaining positive (although these things matter too), but it is about doing what God told you to do despite the circumstances. Being faithful to God and His purpose for your life can get very uncomfortable, but it is necessary.

I had to remain faithful to God during my process. I am a minister and a teacher, so even though I had to spend a lot of time in the hospital, I ministered right there where I was. On the night Mike was medevacked to Washington Hospital Center, despite what was happening in the natural, I had to be faithful to my call and my word. My role in the body of Christ is to minister, so I went to Breezy's Boutique and ministered as scheduled. As believers, we truly need to embody what it means to be faithful to God. We have to stop being fair weather Christians, in other words, serving God and following His instructions when the weather (circumstances) is right, or when we feel like it. That is not being faithful to God, and it is not guaranteeing your reward— the promise – in the end. Just like our processes are all unique, being faithful is different for each person. For someone, being faithful might be committing to serving in a ministry and using their gifts to uplift God's kingdom, versus just coming to church and taking in a Word. For others, being faithful can be prioritizing their life in a way that puts God first instead of last. And for others, it may mean remaining focused on a promise, despite an uncomfortable process. Whatever it is for you, just make a decision to be faithful.

Part of my role in Christ is being a wife first. So while Mike was in the hospital, as a praying and God-fearing wife, my duty was to remain faithful. So I did everything I could to serve God and my husband. Part of my wifely duty was to support my man and let him know that everything was going to be okay. I am called by God to be a help-mate, so to me I am here to assist in meeting his needs. I told you how I brought him crab legs from Red Lobster, right? Well, not only did I go to get the crabs, but I cracked them and fed them to him as well. I had to pick him up at times and put him in a lift. I did not care about what I had to do. It was only temporary, and I was determined to be faithful to what God had called me to do.

When we are faithful, we gain more confidence—not only in ourselves, but also in God's promises to us. If God has told you in His Word that all of His promises are yes and amen, and you know in your heart that you have been faithful, and not fair weather, would not you start believing and trusting God more? If God has already established your end before your beginning, and created you to have life and have it more abundantly, and He's told you that the prayers of the righteous avail much, would you start expecting the best, and expecting your promises from God? Well He has promised you many things, and He has established your end already so what are you going to do with this information? The scripture states, *"For I know the thoughts that I think toward you, says the Lord, thoughts of peace and not of evil, to give you a future and a hope"* (Jeremiah 29:11). Faithfulness is firm devotion to God, loyalty to loved ones, and dependability to carry out responsibilities. Faith is the conviction that even now, God is working and acting on your behalf. If you have faith, and you do, you should also be faithful to God. And I guarantee you that God will demonstrate his faithfulness to you.

To get the best results from your process, do not simply imitate what I did, but imitate my faith and my faithfulness. You cannot and will not get the results that I received if your faith is not truly on fire. Get angry at the enemy, and start reclaiming the things that he stole from you.

Do not be timid.

Do not be scared.

Do not give up when things get hard.

Do not throw in the white flag.

Do not start creating a plan B.

Do not begin begging and pleading for an answer.

Do not turn to your friends for pity.

Do not lose your cool.

Activate your faith by your actions and confessions, and become more faithful and devoted to what you say you believe. If it rains on your parade, put on a rain jacket, pull out your umbrella and parade around worshipping God through the storm. Do not be so easy to give up on what you believe. God will never ever give up on you, and as a matter of fact, He has already put your end in the earth. You will not be able to get the results you want in your life until you can become faithful to the Word in all things. If God told you something, why would He change His mind? God is the same yesterday, as He is today, and will be evermore. Do not allow the enemy to trick you into thinking that just because the situation changed, that God somehow changed. It does not work like that. God is the same. He needs you to be faithful and have faith in knowing that He has done all things. Believe! Believing means standing strong in your faith. Be faithful to God's call for you and the process that He is enabled you to endure.

FAITH PRINCIPLE TWELVE

Do not be a fair weather Christian, up and down depending on the situation. Remember that consistency is key in any relationship. You are now in a committed relationship with God, which means you need to be able to trust Him.

Think about the various roles God has assigned to you. Perhaps you are a parent, leader, entrepreneur, volunteer, daughter or son. How can you be more faithful in those roles as you go about your daily routine? Keep this question on your mind as you serve God and His children.

WORD WEAPON

Stand firm, and you will win life.

Luke 21:19 NIVUK

THIRTEEN
REJOICE, RELAX & REGROUP

So you are out of the process and walking in the promise. Now what? What do you do after your life has been flipped upside down by the most painful situation imaginable and you come out victorious? You rejoice! Praise God! You relax and take a break, and then you regroup and get ready for the next process! You will enter into another process, because life is full of processes. (Remember Genesis 8:22; seedtime and harvest.) The great news is that now that you have been through this process, and you have seen the manifestations of your faith, you have a notch under your belt. You have won. This experience will fortify your strength and your faith even more, because you know that God did it before, and He will do it again. You are going to experience a time when you can simply rejoice at this victory. Maybe your friends and family are rejoicing with you. But after the adrenaline from the victory wears off, you are going to realize how exhausting this experience has been for you. It can be tiring to be in a spiritual fight everyday for an extensive period of time. The crazy thing about this is you do not realize it until you are out of it. That is why you need a strong support system to push you through. Do not give up until you see what you have been in faith for.

As I write this I cannot help but think about a championship athlete who trains for months and months for a race. After crossing that finish line, he looks up and realizes that he is the winner. All of his family and friends, the media, onlookers and fans all celebrate. Everyone is excited and happy. But later that day, or evening, it is time for him or her to take a break! Surely, they are excited and some people may still want him to stay around and celebrate, but it is time for him or her to go rest those muscles, because soon they will have to prepare for yet another race, another process, and more pain in order to experience the next promise.

I want you to be a champion of faith. Spiritually speaking, now is not the time to put your armor down or relax in your preparation. So many people fall into this trap, and get lackadaisical after they have won their battle. People often get away from the same principles of God that got them through. I recently talked with our partners at church about this. People go through a process, and God brings them out of it, and then they get like the children of Israel. God warned them not to forget about Him now that they have made it out. People go through their process, come out as winners, and then they stop going to church like I mentioned earlier. Like clockwork, the devil kicks their butts again. Something else happens, they get desperate, and then they run back to church. The married folks can understand it this way. Before you got married you and your spouse were eager to impress each other and make sure the other person was taken care of. You called regularly, texted cute little messages, and were accommodating to each other's every need. I am sure you remember this phase. But when you got married, you stopped doing those things. The reality kicks in and all of the passion you had in the beginning is gone, and the relationship is in this stagnant, stale place. People do not realize that it takes the same things to keep the relationship healthy once you are in it as it did when you were dating. The same faith principles that got you over that pain and that process will sustain you in the promise, and keep you armed and ready to win the next challenge you will face. We have to exalt the Word everyday, every minute, and every hour, not just when we are going through hard times. Let me challenge you not to get arrogant or prideful and think that you made it through on your own and you do not need God anymore. You will *always* need Him.

As you have read, there have been a series of things that have occurred in my life that have allowed me to stand the way that I stood during my husband's battle. Resting and regrouping after each victory, and continuing to live by faith principles that I chose to use to get me through each battle allowed me to stand strong during the hardest process of my life. You might be thinking about what you are in right now and saying, *"Well I just wasn't prepared for this."* I understand how it feels for something to hit you unexpectedly. However, if you are at this place right now look at my story and embrace it, and know that if you will be determined to trust God, He will bring you over to the other side of this process. If you are not experiencing a tough time right now get prepared through the Word and remain ready so you will have the strength to overcome. Through faith episodes, you can be prepared for anything that will rise.

Just to share, other faith episodes for me were times where members of our church that we truly developed and thought we had relationships with, just walked away from us and threw stones. As you could imagine, people leave churches all the time, and as pastors we have to be prepared for it. Usually it's no big deal. But for those people, whom we had spent a lot of time with and helped the most, to cut us off so unexpectedly, it took a toll on me at one time. You better believe that I hated going through all of what I went through, but when I look back now, I see how I used it as a stepping stone to where I am now. I used every tragedy, hurt, and pain as a weight to anchor me, rather than take me down. A lot of people allow adversity to overtake them. You can let these attacks come and take you out or use them to build you up. The only way for you to use these battles as weights that strengthen you is to truly stay prepared by regularly exercising your faith.

I mentioned the marriage issues that we faced early on, and how at one point, I felt like I was absolutely through with marriage. Eventually, I had to realize that I was not willing to fail at marriage, so my only other option was to begin fighting in faith. Well fighting in faith eventually became living by faith. If I was able to fight for him when our marriage was bad, fighting for him in 2014—after I had been living by faith—was no big deal. Like me, you will begin to see that each battle that you overcome will simply advance you to the next battle. Eventually your trust and faith in God will be so strong that you will not even think about wavering. This is why you have to regroup once you come through. Another challenge lies ahead.

Again, for many people, when we receive victories in our lives, we forget about the One who gave us the victory. I like to call this being in a *faith fight* versus a *faith life*. This is when you activate your faith only during a struggle, versus living this way all the time. Instead, let's use our faith to stay out of the struggle as opposed to always depending on it once we get in a struggle. Let's use our faith to believe God for divine health where we will never get sick, as opposed to having to get sick and depend on faith to get us through. Let's use our faith to raise our children in God's Word, as opposed to using it to save them from disaster because they are not walking in the Word. Do you know faith can prevent some things and save you a world of headaches, right? If we live a faith life, we do not always have to struggle in a faith fight. Romans 1:17 tells us that the just shall *live* by faith.

> *And they overcame him by the blood of the Lamb, and by the word of their testimony; and they loved not their lives unto the death.*
> Revelation 12:11

OUR TESTIMONY

This process yielded another testimony. While Mike was in his healing process I was determined to document everything through video so no one could play down our testimony. From the very beginning I recorded because I knew that God was going to use to this story to bring attention to Himself to show off His healing power. When we returned to our church, Mike had a powerful healing testimony of his own, and the home videos in the hospital that I had taken attracted the attention of news media and church leaders all over the world. Eventually, our story was turned into a documentary, and it has accompanied the lessons that we taught at our own church and at churches across the world.

Even though we are walking in our promise, the journey is not over. And once you make it through, it will not be over for you either. You cannot forget about what you went through. Do not get amnesia, because remembering the works of God, strengthens our faith. Prepare your testimony, and share with others so that they can believe too. The world is waiting on your victory!

Mike had to go to therapy three days a week for about four months when he came home, and he continues to monitor his breathing and the activity in his lungs. Our church partners see us as a walking, living testimony and proof that the faith principles that we have taught for years are God's absolute truth. God wants to be apart of your life at all times, not just during your storms. *Live by faith.* God wants to partner with you everyday and every second of your life to prepare you with the ammunition it will take to win the next war and become the next testimony of unwavering faithfulness. Keep your focus on your promise, go through the process, and never stop living a faith-filled life.

Mike's case is now being used as a case study for medical students. My brother-in-law even met a lady that knew Mike's story from her school assignment. Your story can go down in history so that people whom you have never met can study and learn from what God has done in your life.

FAITH PRINCIPLE THIRTEEN

Rejoice, relax and regroup once you have made it through your process, but do not get comfortable, because there is another process awaiting your arrival. Instead, live by faith and soon nothing will ever be too much for you to handle.

How do you think the processes or experiences you overcame in your past prepared you for your future? One of the best ways to build your faith is to always be ready to pull out the lessons gained from what you have been through. Practice writing about those lessons and sharing them with others. This is your story and hearing your testimonies of faith can help others.

WORD WEAPON

…..I pray for good fortune in everything you do, and for your good health - that your everyday affairs prosper, as well as your soul! I was most happy when some friends arrived and brought the news that you persist in following the way of Truth.

3 John 1:2-3 MSG

STAY FOCUSED.

ABOUT THE AUTHOR

DeeDee Freeman, Founder of Women Walking in the Word

Deloris "DeeDee" Freeman is the wife of Michael A. Freeman, Senior Pastor of Spirit of Faith Christian Center. Devoted to the vision God's vision for the ministry, DeeDee serves alongside to ensure that his assignment is carried out without stress, strain or struggle. An example to women across the body of Christ, DeeDee' leads an inspiring outreach ministry, Women Walking in the Word. DeeDee is a graduate of Liberty University, having earned her Master's Degree in Human Services.

ALSO BY DEEDEE FREEMAN

How a Pastor's wife Can Help or Hurt a Church

Are You a Real Sister Friend

So What! I'm Still God's Glamorous Girl

For more about this book and author, visit:
www.deedeefreeman.com